# Your Rights at Work

Cavendish
Publishing
Limited

London • Sydney • Portland, Oregon

This book is supported by a Companion Website, created to keep titles in the *Pocket Lawyer* series up to date and to provide enhanced resources for readers.

**Key features include:**

◆ forms and letters, in a ready-to-use Word format
  *Access all the material you need at the click of a button*

◆ updates on key developments
  *Your book won't become out of date*

◆ links to useful websites
  *No more fruitless internet searches*

**www.cavendishpublishing.com/pocketlawyer**

# Your Rights at Work

### Bob Watt & Rosy Border

Cavendish
Publishing
Limited

London • Sydney • Portland, Oregon

Second edition first published in Great Britain 2004 by
Cavendish Publishing Limited, The Glass House,
Wharton Street, London WC1X 9PX, United Kingdom
Telephone: + 44 (0)20 7278 8000   Facsimile: + 44 (0)20 7278 8080
Email: info@cavendishpublishing.com
Website: www.cavendishpublishing.com

Published in the United States by Cavendish Publishing
c/o International Specialized Book Services,
5824 NE Hassalo Street, Portland,
Oregon 97213-3644, USA

Published in Australia by Cavendish Publishing (Australia) Pty Ltd
45 Beach Street, Coogee, NSW 2034, Australia
Email: info@cavendishpublishing.com.au
Website: www.cavendishpublishing.com.au

British Library Cataloguing in Publication Data
Watt, Bob, 1953 –
Your rights at work – 2nd ed – (Pocket lawyer)
1 Employee rights – Great Britain – Popular works
I Title  II Border, Rosy
344.4'10101

Library of Congress Cataloguing in Publication Data
Data available

ISBN 1-85941-863-5

1 3 5 7 9 10 8 6 4 2

Printed and bound in Great Britain

# Contents

## PART 3  DISMISSAL AND REDUNDANCY

## PART 4  THE EMPLOYMENT TRIBUNAL AND THE LAW

# Disclaimer

This book puts *you* in control. This is an excellent thing, but it also makes *you* responsible for using it properly. Few washing machine manufacturers will honour their guarantee if you don't follow their 'instructions for use'. In the same way, we are unable to accept liability for any loss arising from mistakes or misunderstandings on your part. So take time to read this book carefully.

Although this book points you in the right direction, reading one small book will not make you an expert, and there are times when you may need to take advice from professionals. This book is not a definitive statement of the law, although we believe it to be accurate as at September 2003.

The authors and publisher cannot accept liability for any advice or material that becomes obsolete due to subsequent changes in the law after publication, although every effort will be made to show any changes in the law that take place after the publication date on the companion website.

# About the authors

**Bob Watt** (BA, BCL (Oxon)) is Senior Lecturer in Law at the University of Essex, where he has taught employment law for 12 years. He is the author of many academic and professional publications. Outside academia, Bob has a young family and when he has time, he enjoys going to the gym and listening to jazz.

**Rosy Border**, co-author of this title and series editor of the *Pocket Lawyer* series, has a first class honours degree in French and has worked in publishing, lecturing, journalism and the law. A prolific author and adapter, she stopped counting after 150 titles. Rosy and her husband, John Rabson, live in rural Suffolk and have a grown up family. Rosy enjoys DIY, entertaining and retail therapy in French markets.

# Acknowledgments

A glance at the 'Useful contacts' will show the many sources we dipped into while writing this book. Thank you, everybody. We would especially like to thank Gill Watt (Mrs Bob) and John Rabson (Mr Rosy) for their support and understanding.

# Welcome

Welcome to *Pocket Lawyer*. Let's face it, the law is a maze and you are likely to get lost unless you have a map. This book is your map through the part of the maze that deals with your rights at work.

## We put *you* in control

This book empowers you. This is a good thing, but being in control means responsibility as well as power, so please use this book properly. Read it with care and don't be afraid to make notes – we have left wide margins for you to do just that. Take your time – do not skip anything:

o   everything is there for a purpose;
o   if anything were unimportant, we would have left it out.

Think of yourself as a driver using a road map. The map tells you the route, but it is up to you to drive carefully along it.

Sometimes you might be in danger of getting out of your depth and you will need to take professional advice. Watch out for the hazard sign.

Sometimes we pause to explain something: the origin of a word, perhaps, or why a particular piece of legislation was passed. You do not need to know these things to make use of this book, but we hope you find them interesting.

Sometimes we stop to empower you to do something. Look out for this sign.

## Clear English rules OK

Client to solicitor who has just drafted a contract for him: 'This *can't* be legal – I can understand it!'

Our style is WYSIWYG – what you see is what you get.

Some legal documents have traditionally been written in archaic language, often known as 'law-speak'. This term also extends to the practice of using the names of legal cases as shorthand for legal concepts. This wording has stood the test of time – often several centuries – and has been hallowed by the courts. Some of the words used sound just like everyday language, but beware – it is a kind of specialist shorthand. When we *do* need to use technical language, we offer clear explanations: see 'Buzzwords', p xv. These words appear in the text in **bold** so you can check their meaning.

## A note on gender

This book is unisex. We acknowledge that there are both male and female members of every group and we try to allow for that in the text by using, wherever possible, the generic *they/them* rather than *he/she, him/her*, etc. Any references to the employer/employee as he/she will, of course, apply to either sex.

## A note on Scotland and Northern Ireland

This book is not wholly reliable for jurisdictions other than England and Wales. Employment law in Scotland is very similar to that in England and Wales, indeed most of the statutes apply to Scotland, but *it is not identical*. For guidance about employment law in Scotland, call ACAS Scotland, on 0141 204 2677. The law in Northern Ireland differs significantly.

## A note on references

By 'references' we mean items like 's 36 of the ERA 1996' which crop up in the text from time to time. These refer to pieces of legislation which are important in this part of the law.

Where possible we have tried to prevent the references from interrupting the flow of the book, but we can't omit them altogether because they are necessary. Where used, 's' is the abbreviation for 'section', and 'ss' for 'sections' of a particular Act.

## Click onto the website

www.cavendishpublishing.com/pocketlawyer

## Getting the most from this book

We aim to tell you all the really important things you need to know and to guide you on the issues where you need to seek professional help and advice. Some matters are far too complex to attempt to solve yourself. We hope that by the time you have read this book you will understand your rights at work. Do remember that the legal process is there as a last resort – know your rights and use them to negotiate with your employer to reach a sensible outcome.

If you follow our advice you should be able to assert your positive rights at work, including:

o  pointing out to your employer that you have a right not to be **unfairly dismissed**;

o  showing your employer that you have a right not to be subjected to unlawful **discrimination** on the grounds of your sex, race or disability;

o  taking a claim to the **employment tribunal** if your employer does unfairly dismiss you, discriminate against you or infringe your rights.

Your positive rights include the right to:

- a safe and healthy working environment;
- a minimum level of pay;
- a limit on the hours you work;
- paid holidays;
- maternity/paternity leave;
- time off to care for dependants.

You also have a legal right to join, or not to join, a trade union, and if you are a trade unionist, you have a right to some representation. Whether or not you are a trade union member, you have a right to be consulted about any changes affecting your employment. We will explain all of these issues.

Only when all else fails is it time to go to the employment tribunal. Consider carefully whether you need to seek professional legal advice before doing so; it is *your* decision.

This book will empower you to take your employer to an employment tribunal, if that is what it takes to assert your rights. The tribunal won't take kindly, however, to being told that you have a particular right, or that your employer has a particular responsibility, unless you say where that information comes from, and you can't just say you read it in our book – they won't be impressed! You need to quote the precise piece of legislation that gives you that right, or your employer that responsibility. You will say 's 36 of the ERA 1996' (or, more fully, 'Section 36 of the Employment Rights Act 1996') and the tribunal will know exactly what you are talking about.

## What this book can do for you

It can give you:

- a practical guide to the main points of employment law;
- the general information that professional advisers would give you on the subject, if only they had the time to do so, and if only you had the money to pay them;

o  the terms, or 'buzzwords' that are important and
   what they mean;

o  answers to some of the most frequently asked
   questions on the subject;

o  access to our companion website, which is regularly
   updated.

## What this book can't do for you

It can't:

o  be a legal textbook;

o  set out a detailed discussion of all the **case law**. The
   leading cases are set out in this book where they
   provide help. **Employment tribunals** are not
   usually very concerned with the details of
   **precedents**; they want to know the facts of each
   case. However, some precedents are very important
   – especially in the area of **discrimination** law – and
   while we give you guidance in these areas,
   sometimes we have to point out that professional
   help is essential.

# Buzzwords

Here are some terms you will come across in this book. Please do not skip this section, as many of the terms used by employment lawyers have special meanings. Here we make them clear. The terms appear in **bold** in the text.

**ACAS** – the Advisory, Conciliation and Arbitration Service. Its stated mission is 'to improve the performance and effectiveness of organisations by providing an independent and impartial service to prevent and resolve disputes and to build harmonious relationships at work' (phew!). A useful range of publications is available from ACAS Reader Limited, PO Box 16, Earl Shilton, Leicester LE9 8ZZ, tel 01455 852225. The ACAS website is at www.acas.org.uk.

If you do take a claim to an **employment tribunal**, ACAS will contact you and will attempt to help you and your former employer to reach an amicable settlement of your dispute. The services of ACAS officers are free and completely impartial, and ACAS professionals themselves are consummate professionals. Do listen to ACAS. We further explain their function and working in Chapter 20, p 141.

**atypical worker** – as opposed to a typical worker, who works, say, from 9 am to 5 pm in 'normal' working conditions, an atypical worker is one whose working hours and conditions are not 'normal'. Examples of atypical workers are homeworkers or casual workers such as fruit pickers, etc. The boundaries between typical and atypical workers are becoming less well defined as more workers adopt more flexible working patterns and the legal protection afforded to atypical workers increases.

**automatically unfair reasons for dismissal** – the law has provided that there are some reasons for which you may not be dismissed without your former employer becoming liable to pay you compensation. These are set out in Chapter 14.

**case law** – 'judge-made' law; **statute** law sets down the rules, and case law documents the ways in which judges have interpreted those rules in ground-breaking cases (see **precedents**).

**collective agreement** – an agreement between an employer and a trade union which, among other things, governs terms and conditions of employment.

**collective bargaining** – the process of reaching a **collective agreement**.

**constructive dismissal** – suppose that you are treated very badly by your employer – for example, he reduces your pay; he redeploys you to a menial job; he insults, demeans or indecently assaults you – and you decide to leave. It sounds like a **resignation**, but the law says that you may have been dismissed, and it is for an **employment tribunal** to decide whether your employer's bad behaviour was sufficient to justify your walking out.

**continuous employment** – the period of time an employee must have worked for an employer before they have certain **statutory** rights. This time period varies with the particular right in question, and we set out in the appropriate place the period of continuous employment which applies to each right. Your period of continuous employment starts with the first day on which you are contracted to work.

**contract of employment** – strictly speaking, a contract of employment is an *agreement* between two legal persons – *an employee* who agrees personally to provide services, and *an employer*, who may be an individual or an organisation such as a company.

The term is often applied to the document more accurately known as a 'Statement of Terms and Conditions of Employment' or a 'Section 1 Statement', but this is incorrect. The contract is the actual *agreement*; the Statement is simply a *record* of what has been agreed. It may well contain errors and is subject to interpretation by the courts.

**contract for services** – an agreement made between an employer and a self-employed contractor.

**contract of service** – an agreement made between an employer and an employee.

**contractual** – set out in a contract, as opposed to **statutory** – laid down by statute. Typically, your **contract of employment** states the statutory rights to which you are entitled by law, but it also gives you additional rights. These are set out in your contract and become 'contractual' rights.

**covenant in restraint of trade** – a promise by the employee, which may continue *after* the employment ends, not to compete with the employer's business (note: covenants in restraint of trade are a legal minefield because you cannot stop someone from earning a living).

**detriment** – disadvantage, damage or harm (for an explanation of detriment in employment law, see Chapter 12).

**discrimination** (**direct**) – less favourable treatment of a person on the grounds of their race or sex or because they are disabled.

**discrimination** (**indirect**) – a condition in a job description which might seem to apply to all, but can actually only be fulfilled by certain applicants for a job.

**dismissal** – an employee is said to be dismissed when his or her **contract of employment** comes to an end. This may be because:

o the employer has brought it to an end with or without notice;

o a short term contract has come to an end and is not renewed;

o the employer has broken the contract of employment and the employee leaves as a result of that breach (see **constructive dismissal**).

**effective date of termination** – the later of 'the day an employee stops working for his employer' or 'the day on which notice runs out'.

**employment tribunal** – a panel, usually consisting of a legally qualified chairman and two lay members, which hears (adjudicates on) employment disputes (you can find out more about employment tribunals in Chapter 20).

**express terms** – the terms written in the **contract of employment** (see also **implied terms**).

**gender reassignment** – a process undertaken under medical supervision with a view to reassigning a person's sex by changing physiological or other characteristics. A transsexual may have had gender reassignment.

**genuine occupational qualifications** – terms which, in normal circumstances, would be considered discriminatory – for example, 'Wanted: a female worker' as opposed to 'Wanted: a worker'. Sometimes a man or a woman, or a person of a specific race, is needed for a job for reasons of decency or authenticity, such as a men's/ladies' changing room attendant or a Nepalese waiter/waitress in a Gurkha restaurant.

**implied terms** – terms not directly stated in the **contract of employment**, either because they are obvious or because they are required for the contract to work properly.

**IRLR** – the *Industrial Relations Law Reports*, the main source of **precedents** used by employment lawyers.

**potentially fair reasons for dismissal** – provided that an employer obeys the law in other respects, they may dismiss you and not be liable to pay compensation if:

o   you are incapable of doing your job;

o   you engage in misconduct;

o   you are **redundant**;

o   keeping you in employment would break the law; or

o   there is some other substantial reason recognised by the law.

**precedent** – a decision of a higher court, such as the Court of Appeal or the House of Lords. The legal reasoning for such a judgment must be followed by other courts and tribunals. It is a *statement of judge-made law*.

'**Precedent**' comes from 'precede': to go before. Precedents are precisely that, and they are a vital part of our legal system. When a legal decision is made which breaks new ground or clarifies a point of law, that decision is recorded as a precedent and will influence future decisions.

**protected disclosure** – a worker can make a protected disclosure – that is, 'blow the whistle' on misbehaviour by an employer – by making a disclosure in good faith of some wrongdoing or alleged wrongdoing to one of the proper listed authorities. If an employer sacks you for making a protected disclosure, it is **automatically unfair** and you are entitled to enhanced compensation.

**protected shop or betting worker** *or* **opted out shop or betting worker** – long standing shop workers or betting workers may have a right not to work on a Sunday. Shop and betting workers may also sign a certificate saying that they do not wish to work on Sundays in general and, provided that they follow the rules, they have protection against being obliged to work on Sundays.

**qualified employee** – in the law of **unfair dismissal**, a qualified employee is one who can bring a case against their employer. In most cases, this means 'an employee who has one year's continuous service'. However, in some special situations – which we describe below – you can bring a claim from the first day of your employment.

**redundant** – briefly and crudely, if you are redundant it means that you are surplus to the employer's requirements for getting the job done:

o    at all; or

o    in the place where you work.

---

Redundancy has a precise legal meaning and is never a means for an employer to get rid of an inconvenient employee. While **redundant** employees are entitled to some compensation, if you think that your employer is just using redundancy as a pretext for getting rid of you, seek professional advice.

---

**re-engagement** – the situation where a tribunal rules that a previously dismissed employee must be given *a* job, but not their original job, with their employer, either on the same or on a different site.

**re-instatement** – where a tribunal rules that a previously dismissed employee should be given back their old job.

**remuneration** – broadly speaking, pay: your fee, salary or wage. However, some elements of compensation for dismissal are also classed as remuneration and this both gives them special protection and makes them liable to tax and National Insurance payments.

**resignation** – where you decide to leave your job. You have no right to any compensation unless this is provided for in your **contract of employment**.

**risk assessment** – where an employer checks out the health and safety risks that exist in their workplace.

**statute** – a piece of legislation, such as the Employment Rights Act 1996. Statute law sets down the rules. Then as cases come up, the judges interpret the law (see **case law**).

**statutory** – laid down by law (for example, **statutory maternity pay**).

**statutory maternity pay** – the legal minimum payment to which a woman taking maternity leave is entitled. Payments are also made in relation to **statutory** paternity pay and the various forms of statutory adoption pay.

**statutory sick pay** – the legal minimum payment to which employees (under the age of 65) who are off work due to sickness for four or more days in a row, including weekends and holidays, are entitled.

**statutory terms** – the terms that are required to be in your **contract of employment** as set down in law.

**summary dismissal** – **dismissal** without notice for reasons such as gross misconduct, where the employer has good reason to do so. Sometimes called 'dismissal without notice and without pay in lieu of notice'. Sometimes employers purport summarily to dismiss an employee where they have no legal right to do so; this may amount to **wrongful dismissal**.

**termination** – the ending of an employee's employment, because the employee resigns or because he or she is dismissed.

**transfer of an undertaking** – where a business or part of a business is sold or transferred to another owner as a going concern. In the public sector, this is often referred to as 'privatisation' or 'contracting out', while in the private sector it usually occurs where an employer decides to change contractors or to transfer some part of the business, for example canteen or cleaning services, to another employer. The basic legal position is that affected employees ought to be transferred to the new employer under the same terms and conditions – the reality is often quite different.

**unfair dismissal** – this is:

○ any **dismissal** which falls outside one of the legal reasons for a dismissal; and which *either*:

– falls outside that which a reasonable employer would do; *or*

– fails to give the employee the benefit of a fair procedure (we give a detailed example in Chapter 16 and refer to two legal cases);

○ any dismissal for a reason which the law says is unfair – for example, you may not be dismissed because you are pregnant, or because you want to join a trade union.

Unfair dismissal is a key idea in employment law and we explain it in detail, with examples, in Chapter 16. In order to bring a claim for unfair dismissal, you must be a **qualified employee**. If you are unfairly dismissed, you may be entitled to compensation.

**vicarious liability** – where the actions and behaviour of employees whilst employed are the liability of the employer. If someone is injured by the action of an employee, the employer may be liable to pay compensation to the injured party.

---

'Vicarious' has more to do with vicars than you might imagine. '*Vicarius*' is Latin for a stand-in or understudy. A vicar is God's (or the bishop's) stand-in. The employee who crashes the firm's van into your garden wall is standing in for the boss, and the law of **vicarious liability** says it is the boss who pays for the repairs.

---

**wrongful dismissal** – in general, you are only qualified to bring a claim for **unfair dismissal** after you have been **continuously employed** for more than 12 months. If you are dismissed *before* the 12-month qualifying period has elapsed, you may be entitled to compensation for wrongful dismissal, but this is limited to the pay that you would have received during your **contractual** notice period. During the first 12 months of your employment your employer can dismiss you without giving any reason and may, unless he does so for certain special reasons, simply act on a whim.

# Frequently asked questions (FAQs)

## How can I take a claim to an employment tribunal?

You start with a form, IT1 (we provide a sample on p 151). Click onto www.employmenttribunals. gov.uk or go to your local Job Centre and ask them for form IT1. Fill it in and either send it online (the website above tells you how, or your local Citizens Advice Bureau (CAB) will help) or post it to the local office of the **employment tribunal**.

*However*, before you do that, do try to resolve your differences with your employer. Show them this book to demonstrate that you know your rights. Make a note of the fact that you have done so, because if your employer is recalcitrant and refuses to grant you your rights, you will have a much better case in the tribunal if you can prove that you did your best to resolve the dispute yourself. Consider carefully whether you want to take independent professional advice before going to the tribunal.

## Does it cost anything to take a case to a tribunal?

If you do it yourself or with the help of your trade union, then the answer is *usually* no. If you engage a solicitor privately, then unless the solicitor is prepared to do it on a 'no-win-no-fee' basis you will have to pay your own legal fees. Also, the rules say 'should you fail to prepare properly for the hearing and as a consequence it becomes necessary to adjourn the hearing you may have to pay costs' (that is, the other side's costs as well as any expenses of your own) – so do your homework first!

However, your former employer may ask for a pre-hearing assessment of the case. This is a sort of 'mini-trial' conducted by a chairman of the tribunal. The chairman will ask questions like 'Does this applicant have a case?' and 'Suppose that everything they allege is true, would they win?'. Then, if the tribunal thinks that you have no reasonable chance of success, they may insist that you pay a deposit. Frankly, if this happens you would do well to consider withdrawing or, at the very least, you should take professional legal advice. If you lose the case, you may lose your deposit.

On the other hand, if you are told that you have an arguable case it may well be that your former employer will ask you if you want to 'settle', that is, resolve the dispute between the two of you without recourse to the tribunal.

## My employers sacked me in 2001. Can I take them to an employment tribunal?

No – or, at least, it is *very* unlikely.

While tribunals do have a very limited discretion to allow people to bring late cases, they do not allow them very often. Although there may be special reasons in a particular situation for allowing a late case to be brought, for the overwhelming majority of employment disputes there is one simple rule.

The 'originating application' (the form making the claim which starts the tribunal process) *must* arrive at the **employment tribunal** *within three months to the day* of the event of which you are complaining. *You must be on time.*

Put a note in your diary to remind you to post the form *at least two weeks* ahead of the closing date.

## What do I do if my employer doesn't give me a contract?

Wait for two months after you start work, then go and ask them for a statement of the main terms and conditions of your employment. Point out that you have a legal right to such a statement (see p 13 for details). Doesn't your employer insist on *his* legal rights, such as the right to be paid by clients for the goods or services he supplies? Why shouldn't *you* have *your* rights respected?

If your employer refuses to play ball, you are entitled to go to an **employment tribunal** to enforce your rights.

## What do I do if my employer won't give me time off because my child is taken ill?

How old is your child? If he or she is under five or has special needs, you may well have a right to parental leave. If it is a sudden illness and you need to take a short period of time away from work, you are entitled to time off. We set out your rights in Chapter 10.

## My employer has accused me of stealing and has told me he is sacking me. I am innocent. What should I do?

On these facts, and assuming that you have the appropriate period of **continuous employment**, go to the Job Centre and ask for form IT1, an originating application to the **employment tribunal**. Fill in the form and submit it (note that the appropriate period of continuous employment to submit a claim for **unfair dismissal** in these circumstances is *one year*. You have almost certainly been unfairly dismissed, and you are entitled to compensation – your employer has treated you badly. Even if you have less than one year's continuous employment, it sounds as though you have been **wrongfully dismissed** (see Chapter 18 for details of your rights).

## My employer has approached me and said that he wants to rearrange my job. He has said that this may involve a substantial downgrading with someone else brought in to do my old job. They would supervise me in my new job. Can he do this?

Can he say that he would like to, or proposes to, rearrange your duties? Yes, he can say that, provided that he:

o  does so in confidence (in other words, not in front of a room full of people);

o  treats you with dignity and respect when he says it; and

o  gives you a clear explanation of the reasons for his proposal.

If he fails in any of these respects, it is likely that you have grounds for an action for **constructive dismissal** (see Chapter 18).

Can he rearrange your duties? Yes, but first, only if your **contract of employment** gives him a clear and unequivocal right to do so. Given the severe consequences of his action upon your terms and conditions of employment generally, and your self-esteem and pay packet in particular, this right would have to be 'clearly and unambiguously set out' in your contract of employment (see Chapter 3).

Perhaps you will agree to your employer's proposals. It may be that you are getting close to retirement age and wish to take things easier, or that your health is poor, or that the new job is part-time and you would like to work part-time. Your employer would then have to issue you with a new contract of employment taking account of the changes you have agreed to.

It is a fundamental of the contract of employment that your employer may *not* unilaterally change your contract without detailed consultation with you. It is a *contract*, a legally binding agreement between equals. If your employer 'just did it' you would almost certainly win an action for constructive dismissal. Suppose, however, that he went through a detailed and reasoned process of consultation and had good, strong business reasons for proposing the change, and you, despite hearing those reasons, refused to consent to those changes – he might then dismiss you and might successfully defend an action for **unfair dismissal**.

## I am handed an envelope at the end of each week with some money in it. Is this right?

Provided that this is not a 'one-off' because your employer's payroll system has crashed (in which case, it is OK just this once), if this is meant to be your wages, there is something very wrong and you must query it.

If you are an employee you are entitled to an itemised pay statement so that you can check that you are receiving the correct amount of pay, that you are not having money unlawfully deducted from your pay and that you are paying the correct amounts of tax and National Insurance (NI). Query it with your employer and if he refuses to give you an itemised pay statement, do challenge the matter in the **employment tribunal**. Quite frankly, if your employer dismisses you for challenging this, you are well out of it – it will just get you more compensation.

Employers who pay you 'out-of-the-till' are not doing you any favours – the authorities are likely to come after *both* of you for tax and NI.

If you are being paid cash-in-hand, you may have fewer legal rights – an **employment tribunal** would be quite entitled to say, 'This is a legally unenforceable contract, as the parties have put themselves outside the law by hiding the matter from the authorities. No tax or NI is being paid. They must go away and fight it out amongst themselves'.

You are probably not getting the national minimum wage either! (See Chapter 5 for your legal rights.)

## My employer does not have a pension scheme. I want to take out a pension but he says that is up to me. Is this right?

It isn't as simple as that. We need more information before we can answer your question. In this situation, as in so many others, your rights depend upon the facts of your individual case.

Having said that (and to put you out of your misery), if your employer has five or more employees they are obliged to offer you a stakeholder pension unless they have an occupational pension scheme. Only if they have fewer than five employees do you have to arrange your own pension.

## I have been off work on maternity leave. I now want to return, but my employer says he has someone else doing my job and doesn't want me back. What do I do?

o   Did you tell your employer that you wanted to take maternity leave?

o   Did you tell him that you wanted to return to work?

o   Have you complied with all the legal requirements? See Chapter 10.

Remember that having *legal rights* means that you have *legal responsibilities* too. You cannot rely on your rights unless you have complied with your responsibilities. If you have, then you can take your employer to the **employment tribunal**. Look at the tailored interactive guidance on employment rights website at www.tiger.gov.uk for details.

**I am registered disabled. I recently applied for a job that I would have had no trouble doing, but I didn't even get interviewed, even though I am very well qualified. I have heard that the person taken on was not as well qualified as I am. I think that I didn't get the job because I am disabled. Is there anything I can do?**

Yes. From the facts you have given us it sounds as though you have suffered **direct discrimination** contrary to the provisions of the Disability Discrimination Act 1995. You may be able to take a claim to the **employment tribunal**.

Furthermore, in discrimination cases the various Commissions may be able to help: the Equal Opportunities Commission, the Commission for Racial Equality, and the Disability Rights Commission, as appropriate (see 'Useful contacts', pp 153–54).

**My employer frequently asks me to work overtime. Sometimes it is difficult but if I try to say no, he says he can always find someone else to do the job. Is there anything I can do?**

Probably not, *unless* your employer is trying to make you work more than 48 hours in a week. If he is expecting you to work more than 48 hours per week, and if you have not opted out of the Working Time Regulations, you do have a claim in the **employment tribunal**. If this is not the case, and your employer is just giving you a lot of hot air, remember that employment law is not an answer to all ills. Look for another job.

**I often work overtime but I never get paid for it. Is this right?**

This depends on your **contract of employment**. Have you agreed to work unpaid overtime? Are you entitled to time off in lieu? Your contract is the key – check it carefully.

**For several years my wife and I have had our name down to adopt a child. Now, at last, six-month-old David is coming to live with us. Is either of us entitled to any leave while he is settling in – and what about later on?**

Yes. In fact, you have the same rights as if you were David's natural parents. Rather than explain here in detail, we refer you to Chapter 10.

**I don't think my workplace is safe. I have spoken to my foreman but he says it's OK. I am worried that sooner or later someone is going to get hurt. What should I do?**

Bring it to the attention of your employer at once; go to a senior manager or to your employer directly. If you are victimised for doing so, you have a right to compensation.

What is more, if you think that the danger is sufficiently serious, go to the Health and Safety Executive. If you are victimised for 'blowing the whistle' you will be entitled to compensation. No one should have to work in a dangerous environment. We set out your rights in Chapter 13.

**I am Jewish, but my employer will not let me have a day off for religious observance on Yom Kippur. Can I take the day off?**

If your employer:

o   is not a public employer; *and*

o   provided that you are not working (as opposed to living) in Northern Ireland (note that it does not matter for the purposes of employment law where you *live* – all employment law rights depend on where you *work*), it is *not* unlawful for an employer to discriminate on the grounds of purely religious affiliation. Some cases have held, however, that to be Jewish is to be a member of an ethnic community and so it may be that you are the victim of racial **discrimination**. (This is not so for Muslims, who are usually seen as a purely religious group.)

Explain to your employer that Yom Kippur is a high holy day and ask them to reconsider. You ought to be allowed to take the day off as holiday or unpaid leave.

## I frequently suffer from racial abuse at work. I have complained to my manager but nothing was done. What else can I do?

Go to your employer and explain that if nothing is done you will have no option but to take the matter to the **employment tribunal**. Your employer will almost certainly be held **vicariously liable** and will have to pay you compensation.

Do keep a diary of all incidents, including dates, the names of those responsible and, however distasteful it may be, the things that are said or done. Note down how you feel about it. If the abuse continues, make an application to the employment tribunal. Your diary will provide useful evidence.

## My boss keeps touching me in a way I find upsetting. I have tried asking him to stop but he says he's just being friendly. What should I do?

Make it absolutely plain that you resent this 'friendliness' and find it completely unacceptable. Keep a note of all the incidents and approach your employer or a senior manager with your complaint. If they do not resolve the situation – if it does not stop or you are victimised – make an application to the **employment tribunal**.

If it was not your employer's wandering hands that offended you but those of a fellow employee, your employer will be held **vicariously liable**. If the wandering hands belonged to your employer, that is your employer's personal liability (see 'Harassment', Chapter 12).

# PART I
# INTRODUCTION

# The history of employment law

Here we set out the changes that have occurred in employment law and the ideas associated with them. If you just want to get to the nitty gritty, we suggest that you skip this section.

## Bryant and May's match girls

Annie Besant campaigned for improved working conditions for the girls who made matches in Bryant and May's London factory. The following article, which appeared in 1888, led to a boycott of Bryant and May's matches and then to a successful strike, which in turn led to changes in the law – see below.

> The hour for commencing work is half-past six in summer and eight in winter; work concludes at six pm. Half an hour is allowed for breakfast and an hour for dinner.

This is now unlawful under the Working Time Regulations 1998 (see p 57). Workers are entitled to place a limit on their working hours and are entitled to reasonable breaks. Young workers, although we do not deal in detail with their rights in this book, are entitled to enhanced protection under regulations derived from the EC Directive on the protection of young people at work (for reference, Council Directive 94/33/EC).

> This long day of work is performed by young girls, who have to stand the whole of the time. A typical case is that of a girl of 16, a piece-worker; she earns

four shillings [20p] a week, and lives with a sister, employed by the same firm, who 'earns good money, as much as eight or nine shillings a week'.

The splendid salary of four shillings is subject to deductions in the shape of fines; if the feet are dirty, or the ground under the bench is left untidy, a fine of threepence [three old pence] is inflicted; for putting 'burnts' – matches that have caught fire during the work – on the bench, one shilling has been forfeited, and one unhappy girl was fined two shillings and sixpence for some unknown crime. If a girl leaves four or five matches on her bench when she goes for a fresh 'frame', she is fined threepence, and in some departments a fine of threepence is inflicted for talking.

These would now be unlawful deductions. We set out your right to wages free from unlawful deductions in Chapter 5.

One girl was fined one shilling for letting the web twist around a machine in the endeavour to save her fingers from being cut, and was sharply told to take care of the machine, 'never mind your fingers'.

You now have the right to a safe and healthy working environment (see Chapter 13).

Another, who carried out these instructions and lost a finger thereby, was left unsupported while she was helpless.

In these more enlightened times she would have been able to sue her employer for compensation. It is likely that the employer would be prosecuted by the Health and Safety Executive.

A very bitter memory survives in the factory. Mr Theodore Bryant, to show his admiration of Mr Gladstone and the greatness of his own public spirit, bethought him to erect a statue to that eminent statesman. In order that his workgirls might have the privilege of contributing, he stopped one shilling each out of their wages,

If this was taken without the workers' consent it would now have been an unlawful deduction (see Chapter 5).

and further deprived them of half a day's work by closing the factory, 'giving them a holiday'. ('We don't want no holidays,' said one of the girls pathetically for, needless to say, the poorer employees of such a firm lose their wages when a holiday is 'given'.)

You now have the right to four weeks' paid holiday each year (see Chapter 9).

So furious were the girls at this cruel plundering, that many went to the unveiling of the statue with stones and bricks in their pockets, and I was conscious of a wish that some of those bricks had made an impression on Mr Bryant's conscience. Later on they surrounded the statue – 'we paid for it', they cried savagely – shouting and yelling, and a gruesome story is told that some cut their arms and let their blood trickle on the marble paid for, in very truth, by their blood ...

Annie Besant was a campaigner for safe and healthy working conditions and was instrumental in controlling the use of phosphorous in matchmaking. However, her forays into theosophy and the more unusual areas of Sanskrit literature have, rather unfortunately, given her a reputation as being somewhat eccentric. Long live eccentricity!

## Charles Dickens: a blacking warehouse in the 1820s

Charles Dickens became one of our most famous novelists, but his education was interrupted because of family poverty. When Charles was aged 12 his father lost his job and was sent to a debtor's prison, and young Charles had to go out to work in a factory which made blacking (shoe polish).

Mr Dickens Senior was the model for Mr Micawber in Charles Dickens's novel *David Copperfield*. Later, when the family fortunes improved, Charles was able to continue his education.

James Lambert, a relative, knowing what our domestic circumstances then were, proposed that I should go into a blacking warehouse, to be as useful as I could, at a salary of six shillings [30p] a week ...

This offer was accepted very willingly by my father and mother, and on a Monday morning I went down to the blacking warehouse to begin my business life.

We do not deal in detail with the rights of young workers in this book, but according to Article 4 of the EC Directive on the protection of young people at work, Council Directive 94/33/EC, children are now prohibited from working save under certain clearly specified conditions. A child is, in the majority of circumstances, a person of less than 15 years of age.

The blacking warehouse was a crazy, tumble-down old house, abutting of course on the river, and literally overrun with rats. Its wainscoted rooms and its rotten floors and staircases, with the old grey rats swarming down in the cellars, and the sounds of their squeaking and scuffling coming up the stairs at all times, and the dirt and decay of the place, rise up visibly before me, as if I were there again.

You now have the right to a safe and healthy working environment. Regulation 9 of the Workplace (Health, Safety and Welfare) Regulations 1992 provides that: 'Every workplace and the furniture, furnishings and fittings therein shall be kept sufficiently clean.'

The counting-house was on the first floor, looking over the coal-barges on the river. There was a recess in it, in which I was to sit and work. My work was to cover the pots of paste-blacking, first with a piece of oil-paper and then with a piece of blue paper, to tie them round with a string, and then to clip the paper close and neat all round, until it looked as smart as a pot of ointment from the apothecary's shop. When a certain number of pots had attained this pitch of perfection, I was to paste on each a printed label, and then go on again with more pots.

No words can express the secret agony of my soul as I felt my early hopes of growing up to be a learned and distinguished man crushed in my breast ... My whole nature was so penetrated with the grief and humiliation of such considerations that, even now I wander desolately back to that time of my life.

The depth of Charles Dickens' despair caused by his work would almost certainly entitle him to claim against his employer if this took place today. Lord Steyn's comments in *Malik v BCCI SA (In Liquidation)* are apposite: 'The relationship of master and servant has been replaced by a partnership in which the employer has taken on some of the responsibility for the physical and psychological welfare of the worker.'

These two short readings demonstrate the appalling conditions endured by workers in the past. Today's legal framework does not permit such things, and no one should feel inhibited from using the law to secure their rights. Clearly, the legal framework did not appear overnight and we trace below some of the important landmarks along the way to the current legal protection. These 'landmarks' are not only legal and historical, but also conceptual. Most of today's talk is about 'rights' and 'duties' and it is true that they are the landmarks in the modern legal and moral landscape. However, it is useful to be reminded that 'rights' are a very recent invention.

## Early regulation and corporatism

Before 1867, the working relationship was regulated by the state, but in an entirely different way from that which we recognise today. The first 'labour law' was introduced in 1349 and was extended into the Statute of Labourers 1350. Why then? The Black Death ravaged Europe and Britain and labour was in short supply. The surviving labourers found that their work was at a premium and they could charge what they wanted for it. More worryingly for the medieval state, for the first time mobility of labour became an issue. The Statute of Labourers 1350, followed by the Statute of Artificers 1563, set up a system of price and wage control and control over labour mobility and training. The rudimentary 'welfare state', controlled by the Parish using the Elizabethan Poor Law, was linked into this apparatus. This system can be seen as an early form of urban corporatism in that the guilds regulated skilled labour and entry into the trade in the towns. In the countryside, labour was regulated by the magistracy. Over time, labour became more militant and legislation was passed to prevent the formation of 'unlawful combinations' designed to raise wages.

This regulation of the early 'trade unions' came to a head in the Combination Acts of 1799 and 1800. The 1799 Act simply outlawed combinations either of employers or employees, whilst the Act of 1800 was far more interesting. Whilst it continued the legal ban on combinations of workers and employers, it also introduced a cheap, summary mode of resolving disputes between masters and servants by introducing arbitration proceedings. Failure to obey the decision of magistrates, who formed the final court of arbitration, could lead to imprisonment for either side. Unfortunately, it did not really work and the Act was repealed in 1824.

The years between 1800 and 1824 really saw the death of the old state-regulated system; one might say that it died in 1824, but failed to fall down until later in the century.

Between 1800 and 1824 the doctrine of 'freedom of contract' rose to its high point. Jeremy Bentham proposed the doctrine that both employers and workers ought to be free to make their own arrangements to buy and sell labour, and this freedom ought to be as great as possible provided that it did not impinge upon the freedoms of others. The doctrines contained in the Combination Acts of 1824 and 1825 made it clear that violence and intimidation as tools of influencing bargains between employers and employees were outlawed, but provided those rules were obeyed, Sir Robert Peel proclaimed that: 'Men who ... have no property except their manual skill and strength ought to be allowed to confer together, if they think fit, for the purposes of determining at what rate they will sell their labour.'

## Freedom of individual contract

Between 1824 and 1867 the doctrine of freedom of contract grew in influence. Regulation was introduced upon industry in the forms of health and safety regulation (dating from as early as 1802 with the Factory Act 'for the health and morals of apprentices and others') and the protection of pay (the Truck Act 1831), but these were essentially measures designed to ensure formal equality in contracts. The Truck Act 1831 remained in force in essence until 1986, and is interesting because it outlawed the payment of wages in kind. Prior to 1831, employees were often paid in goods from the company shop (or 'tommy shop' – hence the expression '*tommyrot*').

'Formal equality in contracts' means simply that the parties were able to agree whatever they liked provided that it did not impede the right of the other party to contract.

## Collective *laissez-faire*

When the medieval system of labour regulation was finally and completely abolished in 1867, this was the highest point of freedom of contract. After 1867, it began to be replaced by another doctrine which was to last until the 1980s. This doctrine was called 'collective *laissez-faire*'.

The trade unions had gained sufficient strength, at least in some trades, to be taken seriously by the employers. The regulation of terms and conditions of work became a matter of negotiation and agreement between trade unions and employers. The unions were concentrated in the skilled, heavy, manual, male trades and terms and conditions were improved there first. 'Women's work', unskilled labour and public service, were under-rewarded until a number of legislative measures improved their conditions in the years between 1890 and 1920. The mechanism by which they did so was interesting; rather than by simply improving the terms and conditions independently, the legislation tied terms and conditions in these trades to those obtained by collective bargaining between unions and employers in the skilled trades. This was the era of the Wages Councils and the Whitley Committees for fixing holidays and hours.

During this period there were upsurges of a new kind of corporatism: agreements between governments, employers and trade unions to run industry in a tripartite way. Agreements were made to regulate labour and wages during the First World War, the Mond-Turner talks of 1928–29, the Second World War, and the Social Contract period of the 1970s. However, from 1945 a new player began to appear: the *individual right*.

## Individual rights

The end of the Second World War ushered in the era of *individual rights*. Individual rights for workers against employers began to be introduced from 1945.

The milestones seem to be the Contracts of Employment Act 1963, the Redundancy Payments Act 1964 and, most notably, the Industrial Relations Act 1971. This last Act introduced, amongst other measures, the framework of unfair dismissal legislation which we still use today. The Equal Pay Act 1970, the Sex Discrimination Act 1975 and the Race Relations Act 1976 are equally part of this legislative framework. (If dates bother you, ignore the dates but take the Acts themselves on board, because they are important.)

During this period, labour rights began to move from being agreed as a matter of negotiation between employers and trade unions, to become the property of individuals. The individual employee, equipped with their individual rights, was able to sue their employer.

This process accelerated and deepened after the election of the Conservative Government in 1979, under Margaret Thatcher. The individualisation of employees' rights against employers was accentuated, and employees gained new rights to sue trade unions as well as employers. Trade unions, too, became legally accountable to their members.

## The move from rights to relationships

Rights are, no doubt, fine things. However, we do not, in any aspect of our lives, go round suing each other each time someone commits a fault against us.

It is at least arguable that the latest developments in employment law reflect a move away from *rights* to a recognition that the important thing about the employment situation is that it is a *relationship*, with give and take, tolerance and respect due to be exercised and acknowledged on both sides. This is a relationship of professionals working together to achieve an aim.

## Mutual respect

The principle that modern employment law – and the modern employment relationship – is a *partnership* has been stated by many people. In his foreword to the White Paper, *Fairness at Work*, which preceded the Employment Relations Act 1999, the Prime Minister, Tony Blair, said:

> This White Paper is part of the Government's programme to replace the notion of conflict between employers and employees with the promotion of *partnership*. My ambition for this White Paper goes far wider than the legal changes we propose. It is nothing less than to change the culture of relations in and at work – and to reflect a new relationship between work and family life [emphasis added].

Notice that this is a departure from 'Old Labour' ideology. Can you imagine Keir Hardy or Clem Attlee asserting that work is a partnership between capital and labour? Tony Blair is now saying that workers and employers have the same interests. This seems to be a fundamental break with the past. The new ideology has led to two sets of developments in the law. First, much more effort is being put into resolving labour disputes before they start, and into providing conciliation and arbitration schemes to resolve them once they *have* begun. Secondly, and we discuss this at length below, considerable effort is going into producing 'family friendly' working practices and policies. This is sometimes known as providing a 'work-life balance', and it includes much more recognition of the family responsibilities of both parents.

As for the future ... well, who can tell? If we speculate about the content of a fresh edition of this book to be written in 20 years' time, we can only say that both the law and the ideology driving the law are likely to have changed. We write for today ...

# 2

# Your rights at work – an explanation

The law provides you with a number of rights at work; gone are the days when you were a 'servant' and your employer was a 'master'.

In this and succeeding chapters we set out your individual rights at work. These include your right:

o  to have a clear statement of your working conditions;

o  to protection for your pay;

o  to regulate your working hours and have paid holidays;

o  to enjoy certain citizenship rights at work;

o  to enjoy maternity/paternity and adoptive leave and to take time off for your dependants;

o  not to be **unfairly dismissed** (and some allied rights);

o  to be free from unlawful **discrimination**; and

o  to a safe and healthy working environment.

Note that part-time, short term and 'out-of-the-till' (casual) workers have not been forgotten. Turn to p 17 for the good news.

## Your individual rights

At the centre of your individual rights at work is your **contract of employment**. All employees have a contract of employment (sometimes called a **contract of service**), for a contract is simply an *agreement* which the courts will enforce. Employees have a special court to enforce their rights – the **employment tribunal**.

Just because your employer has not given you a *written* statement of the main terms and conditions of your work does *not* mean that you do not have a contract of employment. Indeed, the first student misconception law teachers have to correct is that a contract is a piece of paper. A contract is *never* a piece of paper. That piece of paper is a *statement* of the main terms and conditions of your contract – it is strong evidence of some of the things that you and your employer have agreed will govern your relationship.

Many of the terms of your contract of employment are contained in a document which your employer should by law give to you. This is called a 'Section One Statement' (because the right is given under section 1 of the Employment Rights Act 1996), and is what most of us call the 'contract'. We are going to simplify matters: we'll refer to your contract of employment. Purists might not like it, but it's simpler.

Before we start to examine your contract of employment we need to clarify some preliminary points. First, we need to ensure that you are, as a matter of fact and law, an *employee*. Then we will tell you about the various kinds of **contractual** rights that you possess.

## Am I an employee?

Before you are entitled to 'employee's rights' you need to be an employee.

Let's suppose that you work more or less full-time for one person or firm. Clearly, if you have a letter telling you that you are an employee, or a document from your employer headed 'Contract of Employment' or 'Statement of Employment Particulars', you are just about home and dry. Similarly, if your employer is deducting Pay As You Earn (PAYE) tax and National Insurance (NI) payments from your salary, there is little or no problem. In both these cases, you are almost certainly an employee. You work under a **contract of service**, you are entitled to all the rights of an employee and you bear all an employee's obligations. However, the situation becomes more complex if you have agreed to be self-employed and your contract is said to be a **contract for services**. Here you may be a self-employed contractor taking all the risks of your own business, so the question is: are you in business on your own account? Are you, for example, a self-employed builder? The questions for the **employment tribunal** who would decide the case are: (a) Are you economically dependent upon a single employer? (b) Do you take the risks of the business? (c) Are the parties bound by the mutuality of obligation to provide and perform work? If the preponderance of the evidence tends toward the answers (a) yes, (b) no and (c) yes – you will be judged to be an employee. If the answers tend toward (a) no, (b) yes and (c) no, you are much more likely to be an independent contractor.

Problems are much more likely to occur where you don't work on such a regular basis, although even then you could be held to be an employee. The tribunals tend to look at the same tests and focus upon the idea of mutuality of obligation. Do you have to do the work? Can you decide whether to reject it or not and only work if and when you like? If so, you are probably *not* an employee – you contract *for* services. Tour guides commonly fit into this class, as do window cleaners.

If you have a contract of service, you are an employee and are protected by employment rights and have employee's obligations.

If you have a contract for services, you are a self-employed contractor.

## Three kinds of contractual term

There are two basic types of **contractual** term – these are called *express* and *implied*. There is also a third type of term which derives from the collective nature of work, namely *collective rights*. First, we will look at **express** and **implied terms**.

An express term is one which appears in the statement of your contractual terms and conditions, for example, 'You are employed as a widget fabricator'. You have *expressly* agreed to carry out the duties of a widget fabricator. Express terms are to be found in the **contract of employment** and in the documents expressly affixed to that contract.

Whilst *express* terms and conditions seem at first sight to form the most important part of the contract of employment, this is not, in fact, the case. Lying behind that piece of paper (if it exists) are a number of *implied* terms. These implied terms have a number of sources.

First, there are implied terms which the tribunals will assume that you and your employer have agreed as a matter of course, to make the contract work. Tribunals often refer to 'business efficacy' – all they mean by this is that the contract does what it is supposed to do. The contract simply could not work without these terms having been agreed. Suppose, for example, you get a job as a van driver. Everyone looking at the contract would say, as a matter of common sense, 'Well, you have got a current driving licence, haven't you?'. A term that you have a licence would be *implied* into the contract. Clearly, such a term is specific to you as a driver – your workmate who uses a computer in the office does not need to have a driving licence to do their job.

Secondly, there are terms of *general implication*, which are *implied* into everyone's contract of employment. These come from the general law and are enforced by the courts. They fall into two classes:

o    the common law class – made up of **precedents** set by the judges; and

o    the **statute** law class – legislation made by parliament.

When it comes to 'everyday workers' rights in practice' – those things upon which you rely in your daily working life – the most important group by far is the set of **statutory** rights. These are set out in Chapters 5–14.

The rights implied by the judges (precedents) will not, in the main, concern you nearly so much except in one supremely important case – *the right to have the employer maintain mutual trust and confidence.* We set out the main common law rights and duties and focus upon this most important matter in Chapter 4.

Finally, we move to *collective rights*. Somewhere in your contract of employment, you will find a term saying *either*:

o  'The employer recognises the General Trade Union as conducting **collective bargaining** on behalf of workers in your grade'; *or*

o  'No **collective agreements** apply to your contract'.

In the first instance, this means that certain terms and conditions relating to your contract are fixed by negotiation and agreement between a trade union – whether or not you are a member – and your employer. These fall into two main classes – those terms and conditions which properly form part of your contract, such as pay, hours and holidays, and those which do not, such as mechanisms for negotiation between the union and your employer. Intermediate terms, such as **redundancy** agreements, give lawyers and the courts lots of trouble trying to decide exactly which side of the line they lie. You will never have to fight these battles yourself – they form the legal battleground between employers and trade unions.

So, in Chapter 3 we look at the contract of employment – the express terms and conditions of your contract.

## Part-time, short term, 'out-of-the-till' and 'casual' workers

Sometimes an employer will claim that employment rights do not apply to you because you are a part-time, short term or 'casual' worker. They are quite wrong.

Many people begin their working lives by delivering newspapers. Certainly newsboys and newsgirls are part-time – usually working no more than half to one hour on six or seven days each week. They are short term – filling in the time between their 14th birthday and (at the most) going to university at the age of 18. They are almost always paid 'out-of-the-till', and they form part of the newsagent's accountant's annual nightmare – getting the books in order for the end of the tax year. Are they casual? Often they set their own working times, arrange their own routes, bring their own bikes and organise their own holiday relief.

Whilst the matter of holidays is extremely fraught (and at the time of writing a case is about to go to the Court of Appeal on this matter), it is quite clear that newsboys and newsgirls are employees, and thus are entitled to many of the rights of all employees. The two rights to which they are not generally entitled – paid holidays and wage regulation (the national minimum wage) – are excluded, not by some quirk of their employment status, but simply because of their age:

o    employees below school leaving age are excluded from the right to four weeks' paid holiday by the Working Time Regulations 1998 (see p 57);

o    the national minimum wage does not apply to people under the age of 18.

At the time of writing, however, both of these rules are being tested in the courts. Newsboys (so far as we know, they have all been boys so far) have won cases in **employment tribunals** challenging the fairness of their dismissals and, because only employees can use employment tribunals, the tribunals have confirmed in passing that the newsboys are employees.

Accordingly, there is no exclusion from employment rights for part-time, short term, 'out-of-the-till', or 'casual' employees *provided that* they meet the general definition of employees given above.

## Part-time and short term

Indeed, the general case is that part-time and fixed term workers have to be treated *equally* with full-time workers. The law is to be found in the Part-time Workers (Prevention of Less Favourable Treatment) Regulations 2000, as amended and the Fixed term Employees (Prevention of Less Favourable Treatment) Regulations 2002.

The Part-time Workers Regulations provide that part-timers should not be treated less favourably than full-timers unless it is *objectively justified* (see below). This means that they should receive:

o    the same hourly rate of pay;

o    the same access to company pension schemes;

o   the same entitlements to annual leave and maternity/paternity/adoption and parental leave on a *pro-rata* basis (that is, half the leave if they are employed half-time, and so on);

o   the same entitlement to **contractual** sick pay; and

o   the same access to training opportunities

as full-time employees. Your employer cannot simply say, 'You are part-time, therefore you receive less favourable terms and conditions than a full-timer'.

---

This law is quite new and has not yet 'taken root'. The rules about 'objective justification' of differences are complex and you should seek professional advice before taking legal action.

---

What is meant by 'objective justification'? The rules for objective justification seem to derive from a case before the European Court of Justice called *Bilka-Kaufhaus*. They hold that the employer has to have a legitimate goal and that the means chosen to reach that goal (that is, affording you lesser rights) are both *necessary* to reach that goal and are *proportionate* (appropriate) to that goal. So the employer has to have a sound and legitimate business case and must be acting proportionately and fairly. At the time of writing, it is difficult to give examples of objective justification for treating part-time workers less favourably, because no cases have yet come before the courts.

The Fixed term Employees Regulations came into force in October 2002. Again, they give fixed term employees the right to the same treatment as permanent employees. The essence of the law turns on *comparability*. You must find a *comparator* employed by the same employer at the same or another place of work:

o   who has broadly the same skills and qualifications; and

o   who is doing broadly the same work.

The law applies to employees on contracts that last for a specified period of time or that end when:

o   a specified task (such as building a supermarket or setting up a database) has been completed; or

o   a specified event does or does not happen (for example, maternity leave cover).

# Fixed term employees

Fixed term employees should not be treated less favourably than comparable permanent employees merely because they are fixed-term employees, unless this is objectively justified (see above).

Clearly, the comparison of employment packages between employees can be tricky and the Regulations provide two means of comparison – either:

o    a point-by-point direct comparison of terms and conditions – Ms A (permanent) is paid £10 per hour, thus Ms B (fixed-term) should be paid £10 per hour; or

o    a broad balancing test – Ms A gets £10 per hour for a fixed working week, but Ms B gets £9.50 on a job-and-finish basis (that is, a job where she can go home when she has completed her workload for the day).

A fixed-term employee has the right to ask their employer for a written statement setting out the reasons for any less favourable treatment. The employer must provide this statement within 21 days.

We have all met people who work for long periods for the same organisation on a series of short term contracts, while supposedly 'permanent' workers come and go. Under the new legislation, the use of successive fixed-term contracts will normally be limited to four years (although there is room for genuine negotiation on this matter) and generally, if a fixed-term contract is renewed after the four-year period, it will normally be treated as a permanent contract.

When this happens, a (formerly) fixed-term employee has a right to ask their employer for a written statement *either:*

o    confirming that their contract is now permanent; *or*

o    setting out the objective reasons for the use of a fixed-term contract beyond the four-year period.

Again, the employer must provide this statement within 21 days.

If you believe that you are being less favourably treated than a permanent employee because you are on a fixed-term contract, or that your rights have been infringed, you can take your case to an **employment tribunal**.

---

At the time of writing, this law is quite new and not yet 'run in'. The rules relating to 'objective justification' of differences are complex and you should seek professional advice before taking legal action on any of these matters.

---

## 'Out-of-the-till' and 'casual'

Do check pp 14–15, where we set out the difference between an *employee* and a *self-employed contractor*. If you are an employee you have the right to be treated as an employee; you are *not* a slave. As we have shown, you have the right to at least a minimum level of pay, statutory holidays and lawful and decent conditions of service.

The courts have had to deal with the question of **atypical** workers in a number of cases where 'casuals' are concerned. In a case called *Carmichael,* the House of Lords considered the case of a woman who, from time to time, was contacted by the operators of a local power station to give guided tours. She was completely free to accept or decline the work. The question for the court was 'is she an employee, entitled to paid holidays?'. The answer was 'no – because she was only an employee for the very short periods she was actually working – the contract of employment did not exist between tours. However, it must be noted that she did work for very short periods; holiday entitlements do start from day one of employment. If your employment is for appreciable periods you are entitled to statutory protection of hours and holidays.

# Your contract of employment

According to s 1 of the Employment Rights Act 1996 you are entitled to a written statement of the terms and conditions of employment within two months of starting work for an employer. The law provides that this statement may be given to you in instalments. It sets down that it must contain certain information. We set out a **contract of employment** below, together with some commentary explaining what you will find in the contract and how it affects your rights at work.

## Statement of Employment Particulars – Pursuant to Section 1 of the Employment Rights Act 1996

The title of the document is not especially significant: it may well say 'Contract of Employment'. However, technically it is only very strong evidence of the terms and conditions of your **contract of employment**. It may be that either you or your employer can show that the actual agreement to which you are working is significantly different from that which is set out in the document.

### The Employer's name is

This should be the registered name of your employer. If – and everyone hopes that this never comes about – you need to take legal action against your employer, this is the name in which they should be sued.

## The Employee's name is

Your name.

## This employment began/will begin on

Make sure this date is correct. It is very important for the calculation of your period of **continuous employment** which affects:

- o your right to compensation for **unfair dismissal**;
- o how much redundancy pay you are entitled to if you are made **redundant**;
- o your rights to various forms of **statutory** pay and leave – maternity/paternity, adoptive and sickness;
- o your rights, if any, to **contractual** pay for sickness, etc.

## The period of continuous employment (taking into account any employment with a previous employer which counts towards this service) began/will begin on

Make sure this date is correct – it is very important for the calculation of your period of **continuous employment**. It could be that you have transferred from another linked employer or that your employer has been taken over.

## The remuneration for this post is

**Remuneration**, broadly speaking, is pay. Your employer should set out:

- o your rate of pay; *and*
- o the intervals between pay cheques (weekly, monthly, etc).

Remember that the National Minimum Wage Act 1998 sets out a *minimum wage* (NMW). This is at the time of writing:

- o £4.50 per hour if you are 22 years old or older;
- o £3.80 per hour from your 18th to your 22nd birthday;
- o £3.80 per hour if you are 22 years old or older and on accredited training.

## Your normal hours of work are

Remember that your employer is not allowed to *insist* on your working more than 48 hours in any week unless you are in one of the exempt classes of workers (such as hospital doctors and HGV drivers). They can, of course, ask nicely and make it worth your while; this is something to be agreed between you. This right is to be found in the Working Time Regulations 1998 (see p 57).

## Your entitlement to paid holiday is

Remember that the Working Time Regulations 1998 entitle you to *20 working days' paid leave in each full year*. Your entitlement to paid leave starts on your first day of work, but there is an accrual period during your first year during which you 'earn' your paid holiday:

o     if you work full-time (five days per week) you have to work for approximately three and a half weeks in order to earn one day of paid leave.

You should also expect to find a statement of the number of days' public (Bank) holidays to which you are entitled in addition to your four weeks' paid leave.

Your employer must give you an indication of how pay in lieu of holiday not taken will be calculated when you leave.

## If you are absent from work due to sickness or injury

Here you will usually find a statement along the following lines:

> You should arrange for the Company to be informed by telephone by noon on the first day of absence. You are required to self-certificate for absence due to sickness of four days or less. For periods in excess of four working days a doctor's certificate is required.

This means letting your employer know by noon on the first day you are off sick, and providing your own explanation for absences of four days or less. After four days, you need to provide a medical certificate explaining why you are unable to work.

Many employers add a statement to the effect that: 'The Company reserves the right to terminate your employment with notice after three months of continuous absence due to sickness.'

## The Company (does not) operate(s) a sick pay or maternity pay scheme in advance of the statutory sick pay (SSP) or statutory maternity pay (SMP) schemes

Here you will find details of your employer's sick pay and maternity pay schemes. Your employer has no obligation to operate an occupational scheme and may simply refer you to the government's own SSP and SMP arrangements. Some useful guidance on maternity/paternity rights and adoption rights is to be found at www.tiger.gov.uk (the tailored interactive guidance on employment rights website). This website also contains ready-reckoners to calculate the minimum statutory entitlement. However, do be aware that the state schemes are the legal *minimum*; your employer may offer you more.

### Pension scheme details

The government pension website at www.pensionguide. gov.uk says: 'The Government believes that the best way for you to have a secure retirement is to use the basic state retirement pension as a start. If you want to increase your pension for when you retire, you need to think about the best additional or second pension option for you. The earlier you start paying into a pension and the more you pay in, the higher your pension will be.'

There is a range of pension options available in addition to the state retirement pension:

(a) Provided that you earn more than the lower earnings limit, you are entitled to the State Earnings Related Pension (SERPS) if your employer does not run a contracted out occupational pension scheme.

(b) Your employer may run an occupational pension scheme, which may be in addition to SERPS or contracted out of it. Contracted out schemes mean that you have to pay a lower NI contribution. The benefits of these schemes are usually high, but they are relatively expensive for both employers and employees.

(c) If your employer has more than five employees, the Welfare Reform and Pensions Act 1999 obliges him or her to make a *stakeholder* pension available to you. These are low cost private pension schemes.

(d) If you work for a very small employer, it may be that a private pension scheme is all that is available to you. You should always take independent financial advice before entering a private pension plan.

---

Forget 'financial advisers' on commission until you have obtained the most basic advice. You may wish to go to one later – it's *your* choice. The government website at www.pensionguide.gov.uk is the first place to turn for basic advice, and it's free!

---

## Notice clause

Section 86 of the Employment Rights Act 1996 sets out the rights of the employer and the employee to minimum periods of notice. No **contract of employment** may routinely require periods of *less than* those set out to be given to employers or employees; however, the employer and employee may *agree* to vary the period or to accept payment in lieu of notice.

Here are those minimum notice periods:

o An employee with *less than two years'* **continuous service** is entitled to *one week's notice*.

o An employee with *more than two years' but less than 12 years'* continuous service is entitled to *one week's notice per year of service*.

o An employee with *more than 12 years'* continuous service is entitled to *12 weeks' notice*.

An employer:

o is entitled to one week's notice from an employee, if the employee has more than one month's continuous service.

Note, however, that these are *minimum* periods of notice – most contracts of employment contain an agreement for longer periods of notice, especially from the employee. This is quite lawful.

### The job title is

Here you should find your job title and grade.

### A brief description of the work you are employed to do is

Most large and many small employers provide a job description. This may be set in accordance with an analytical job evaluation programme or it may be a simple note of your main duties. The job description may even refer to the job advertisement.

If the job description in your employment contract refers to the advertisement for the post, keep a copy of the ad safely.

### This employment is intended to be permanent/for a fixed term which will terminate on

This is self-explanatory. Do remember that just because your job is only designed to last for a fixed term, the terms and conditions of employment should be comparable with those of permanent workers.

### Your normal place of work

The standard term you should expect here is:

> is Work House, 1–2 Station Road, Anytown, Anyshire AN1 1AA. You may be required to move your place of work within a 10-mile radius of Anytown Town Hall without notice on a temporary or permanent basis. You may be required to move outside this area on a temporary basis at one week's notice or, upon one month's notice, permanently.

### There are (no) collective agreements affecting the terms and conditions of this agreement

Some **contracts of employment** contain terms and conditions which are negotiated between a trade union, whether or not you are a member, and your employer. These commonly include such fundamental terms as pay, holidays and hours of work. If you find a term here such as 'Acme plc recognises the General and Special

Union as the **collective bargaining** agent for staff employed on your grade', you may wish to consider joining the union. It is your free choice; no one may compel you to join or not to join a particular union or any trade union at all. Moreover, you cannot be penalised for not joining.

## You are (not) required to work outside the United Kingdom

If you are required to work outside the UK, your employer must give you information regarding:

o   the period of such work;

o   the amount of **remuneration** and any bonus payable; and

o   the arrangements for return to the UK.

## Disciplinary code

From time to time, employers may become dissatisfied with their employee's work or conduct and may wish to take disciplinary action. This is action designed to remind the employee of the standards expected from them, and intended to show the employee how to reach and maintain those standards.

Employers are now obliged by the Employment Act 2002, which amends the Employment Rights Act 1996, to provide all employees with the protection of a basic disciplinary code which sets out a minimal fair procedure for investigating and dealing with disciplinary issues. If they fail to do this and they discipline you in a way which fails to come up to the minimum standards of the code, the **dismissal** will be **unfair**. However, if the procedure used is in compliance with the minimum standards you will not be able to complain that the employer acted unfairly.

Thus, you should expect to find a copy of the disciplinary code attached to your Statement or you should be referred to its whereabouts.

## Grievance procedure

It cuts both ways: an employee may not be happy about their treatment at work. The grievance procedure is designed to allow disputes and grievances to be sorted out amicably.

## Other terms and conditions

The information set out above is fundamental to a **contract of employment**.

There may well be other **express terms** of the contract of employment which are included in the document.

Remember, however, that these express terms amount only to strong evidence of what has been agreed between you and your employer. It may be that you and your employer have, in fact, agreed something else but neither of you has taken the trouble to record it. Whilst this is bad practice, it does happen. For example, suppose that the employer has inserted a term into the contract: 'No alcohol may be consumed on the premises.' This is a perfectly sensible term of the contract to which everyone would agree because there is machinery at work. However, the employer has a tradition that at Christmas, *after the machines have been turned off*, he gives everyone a glass of sherry and a mince pie. No one would think that this was silly either. The problem is that it *seems* to break the contract. However, *it does not* – the contract has been varied with the agreement of both sides.

The kinds of terms one would normally expect to see here are as follows:

### Conduct code

This usually covers 'works rules' such as:

o    dealing with customers;
o    dealing with colleagues;
o    dress code;
o    the use of the telephone and the internet at work.

## Equal opportunities code

Policy and procedures for dealing with:

o    equality of opportunity;

o    anti-**discrimination** rules and anti-harassment rules;

o    ensuring that, for example, spouses/partners are not responsible for grading or promotion decisions concerning each other.

## Managing absence due to sickness procedure

Your employer does have a right to manage sick leave – for example, by asking you questions about uncertificated sick leave and regular certificated leave. This is as much for your protection as your employer's – is your work making you ill?

## Compassionate leave policy

What arrangements are there for compassionate leave? Your employer may have a policy for dealing with compassionate leave. Remember that you do have a right to unpaid time off for dealing with emergencies affecting dependants.

## Confidentiality, restraint of trade and non-solicitation clauses

Sometimes employers insist upon the confidentiality of trade secrets. This is a lawful and legitimate concern and the **case law** shows that the courts will protect employers' interests in this respect.

However, sometimes employers try to prevent you from working for a competitor or from setting up your own business after you have left their employ. The law recognises that people must be allowed to earn their living, and it often strikes out **covenants in restraint of trade**. A non-solicitation clause attempts to prevent you tempting customers away from your old employer to your new one.

In other words, to put it quite bluntly, your employer is allowed to try it on – but may have trouble making it stick!

### Collectively agreed terms

Some terms of a **contract of employment** are 'collectively agreed', that is to say, agreed between a trade union representing employees, whether or not they are members of that or any other trade union, and an employer or employers' association.

The most common type of term deals with pay or hours and holidays. A **collective agreement** is not usually *enforceable* as such. This means that if an employer agrees a pay rise with a trade union, or a trade union agrees with an employer not to strike, neither side may sue the other for breaking the agreement.

However, an *individual* employee can sue an employer for unpaid wages due under a collective agreement, if the employee can show that the term in question was incorporated into the employee's individual contract of employment.

Actually demonstrating that a term from a **collective agreement** has been incorporated into your **contract of employment** is tricky. Seek professional legal advice before starting to litigate.

'Litigate' comes from the Latin '*litigare*': to go to law, and a litigant in person is someone who does this without being represented by a lawyer.

# 4

# Your relationship with your employer

In this short chapter we deal with the leading obligation placed on employers (and employees) – the maintenance of mutual trust and confidence. This is the **implied term** *par excellence*. Trust one another. Have confidence in one another.

Labour lawyers, and labour law students in particular, can tell you that they readily spend some 15 hours of study looking at the implied obligations contained in the **contract of employment**; fortunately we can have a much more brief discussion here.

One of the leading academic commentators on employment law, Douglas Brodie, has identified the maintenance of mutual trust and confidence as central to the workplace relationship. He calls it 'the heart of the matter' and we adopt this term.

Our discussion of the matter may seem a little odd at first sight because we deal with cases in which 'the heart is broken'. This is part of the difficulty with law – just as medicine seems to deal in the main with illness rather than health, law seems mostly to deal with things when they go wrong rather than when they are proceeding smoothly and happily; few happily married couples consult a lawyer about their marriage! However, you will find that our discussion also illustrates how people can work to get things right and maintain a good working relationship.

The courts and tribunals have long been faced with cases in which the employer has behaved badly towards an employee.

- In one famous case, the employer said at a woman employee's hearing, 'She can be an absolute bitch on a Monday morning'.

- In another case, a foreman and another worker picked a female employee up off the ground and the foreman put his hand up the woman's skirt. This is an example of **vicarious liability** – the employer was liable for his employees' behaviour.

- More prosaically, an employee was demoted from a responsible position to a junior post where most of her duties appeared to consist of cleaning.

- And what about the man who was told to move his place of work more than 100 miles on the following Monday morning?

- Or the blameless employees of the major bank whose name became a byword for corrupt dealing, who found themselves unable to get another job because other employers said, 'You were a fund manager for X Bank, so you must be a crook ... we are not going to employ you'?

Two final examples will suffice – how would you feel if you worked for a local council and one of the councillors called you 'a lying toerag'? Or if you worked in a children's home and you were accused by a child of committing an assault which you could not possibly have committed – the allegation was absurd – but nevertheless you were suspended from work while the case was investigated?

All these examples are taken from **case law** and, whilst they are extreme and the overwhelming majority of employers would never behave like that, they are all examples of the employer failing to abide by this central obligation.

To redress the balance a little, and to show too that there are some employees from hell, what about the cathedral organist who pocketed concert fees, or the scientific instrument technicians who, in their spare time, went into competition with their employer? Did they act in a way that would maintain the employer's trust and confidence in them? The only rational answer must be 'no'.

So how does this 'cash in' as practical advice? It reveals something important about the nature of the employment relationship. Preserving the working relationship, like most human relationships, is based upon mutual trust and confidence. Both parties have to put some effort into maintaining the relationship and so this means allowing some give and take on both sides.

In fact, the concept of 'sides' is completely alien to this notion of partnership. Clearly you do not go to work to be exploited, but neither do you have the right to exploit your employer. Then look again at the examples we have set out above, and notice the outrageousness of these people's behaviour. Imagine if a man called a woman a 'bitch' in the street, or indecently assaulted her. The police would be involved. Demoting a person, or forcing them to disrupt their home and their children's schooling by changing their duties at short notice without consultation, must break the relationship.

The courts and tribunals have repeatedly emphasised that only major problems are sufficient to break the relationship. The examples we have just quoted were major incidents, but read on.

Imagine some alternative facts: where a man was abusive to a woman in the workplace and, following her complaint, the management took immediate action and tried to get her co-operation to discipline the wrongdoer. She refused to co-operate and resigned instead, saying that the employer had destroyed the relationship. She sued for **constructive dismissal**. No, said the tribunal, what happened was deeply to be regretted but the employer tried, in good faith, to put things right.

To take another example, where an employer planned to move their base of operation and started consulting with the employee in good time about the move, offering him temporary accommodation and help with moving expenses and school transfers – the employee failed in his claim that the employer had breached the central 'trust and confidence' clause of their contract.

So our point is clear: the concept of implied trust and confidence sits at the heart of the contract of employment and serves to remind both parties to act in a civilised and humane manner. *Consult, discuss and raise issues of concern in a proper and sensible manner.* Furthermore, we should point out that the vast majority of working relationships start, progress, and come to an end without the trust and confidence term ever being brought into question. Most people do not notice it, any more than anyone is aware of their healthy heart beating steadily every second of every day.

Incidentally, it is this clause which demonstrates the clear difference between a **contract of service** (the employment contract) and the **contract for services** (the contract of an independent contractor). Independent contractors expect to be exploited to some extent – they charge for the exploitation!

# PART 2
# YOUR RIGHTS

# 5

# The protection of wages

In this and succeeding chapters, we will go through your **statutory** rights. Most, but not all, of these rights derive from the Employment Rights Act 1996 as it has been amended over the years. Some other pieces of legislation contain important employment rights and we have included these in our discussion.

Why don't we have one all-inclusive 'one Act' Labour Code? Why indeed? Why isn't the whole of English law like that? Because the law evolves gradually. In the context of employment law, successive governments keep changing the law according to differing political needs, and sometimes these needs are broader than the confines of labour law.

## Your right to a statement of the main terms and conditions of your contract of employment

First, please recall that all employees have a **contract of employment** or a **contract of service**. A contract is simply an *agreement* which the courts can enforce. Employees have a special court called an **employment tribunal** to enforce their rights as employees.

Part I of the Employment Rights Act 1996 gives you a right to particulars of your employment.

o  You have a right to a written statement of the main terms and conditions of your contract of employment. Your employer must provide this within two months of your starting work (s 1).

o  You have a right to a written statement of any changes to your contract of employment (s 4).

o    If your employer fails to give you such a statement, you may apply to an employment tribunal for an order determining the particulars which ought to be included in such a statement.

While the employer ought to provide you with a statement and would be liable to pay you compensation if they dismissed you for insisting upon your right to be given one, it is difficult to see what could be gained by going to the tribunal *merely* to obtain the statement. However, if you are victimised by being dismissed for bringing such an action, this is **automatically unfair** under s 104 of the Act and you do not need the qualifying period of one year's **continuous employment** in order to bring a claim.

The real usefulness of this action is to be found in its combination with an action for **constructive** or **unfair dismissal**. Suppose that you were employed by the employer for one purpose and then your job was altered, usually by being downgraded, without your consent. You would undoubtedly complain and your employer might respond by dismissing you. You could then use the right set out above.

In such circumstances, it is likely that your employer would not give you the written statement of reasons for dismissal (to which you are entitled under s 86; the enforcement power is given by s 91). Use these two rights in combination with your action for unfair dismissal.

---

Remember, if you are not supplied with a detailed job description, make sure that you keep a copy of the original job advertisement and any other details you are given.

---

## Protection of wages

Part II of the Employment Rights Act 1996 gives you the right to have your wages protected. You have a right to an itemised pay slip which tells you:

o    how much you have earned before any deductions have been made;

o the amount of any deductions (tax, National Insurance (NI), pension);

o the actual amount of money you have been paid; and

o how (for example, by cheque) that money is paid to you (s 8).

Your employer may not make any deduction from your wages unless:

o it is required by law (tax, NI or, for example, a court order for attachment of earnings); *or*

o it is agreed to in the **contract of employment** (for example, pension contributions); *or*

o it has been agreed to in writing by you (because, for example, you wish to make regular donations to charity or to pay a subscription to the works social club) (s 13).

You are not required to make any payment to your employer unless you have agreed to do so, either in your contract of employment or if you have given specific written permission for such a payment to be made (s 15). Hang on – why should you pay your employer? Well, it can happen; for example, suppose you are buying a car from your employer, or paying the fees for the works nursery.

Special provisions do apply to the overpayment of wages and expenses, and your employer may, it seems, just deduct any overpayment from your next wage packet without needing to ask. This provision also applies where the overpayment of wages was due to your being on strike.

If you work in retail employment (such as in a shop), your employer is allowed to dock your wages in respect of cash shortages (if your till roll does not tally with the takings) or stock shortages (if the number of items left is less than expected on a stock check). An employer may not do this, however, unless they can show *either*:

o that your conduct as an employee was dishonest or in some way contributed to the loss (such as handing the customer the wrong change); *or*

o that such a deduction was agreed in your contract of employment (s 17).

Any such deduction for shortage must be made within one year of the discovery of the shortage, and must not exceed one-tenth of the total (before any deductions) amount of wages/salary payable on that day (s 18).

If your employer docks your pay without a proper reason, you may complain to an **employment tribunal** for redress and they may order the employer to make good the unauthorised deduction. If you are victimised by being dismissed for bringing such an action, this is **automatically unfair** under s 104 of the Act and you do not need the qualifying period of one year's **continuous employment** in order to bring the claim.

The other vital thing to remember in the matter of wage protection is the substantive protection of wages set out in the National Minimum Wage Act 1998. At the time of writing, the rates guaranteed are:

o    £4.50 per hour if you are 22 years old or older;

o    £3.80 per hour from your 18th to your 22nd birthday;

o    £3.80 per hour if you are 22 years old or older and on accredited training.

The National Minimum Wage is updated from time to time; you can check the current rate at www.tiger.gov.uk (the tailored interactive guidance on employment rights website).

## Guarantee payments

Part III of the Employment Rights Act 1996 gives you the right to a guarantee payment – the right to some pay if your employer cannot provide you with work provided that you have been continuously employed for one month, or – if you work on a short term contract said to be less than three months' duration and you have, as a matter of fact, worked more – you have the right to be paid your normal day's pay even if your employer runs out of work for you to do or if something happens to stop you working (for example, the factory burns down).

Interestingly, this entitlement to 'a normal day's pay' is currently limited to the sum of £17.30 and is normally limited to a period of five days in any three-month period. So, as anyone would expect to earn more than £86.50 in three months(!), you will be seriously out of pocket (ss 28–31). However, this is very unlikely to come about, because the right to a *guarantee payment* does not take away your right to *any* **contractual** *payment* – the money your **contract of employment** says you are entitled to.

If your contractual right to payment provides more money than this – and if it doesn't, you should look for another job! – your contract of employment kicks in. The overwhelming majority of modern contracts of employment provide that you shall be paid whether or not the employer has any work for you to do, usually because the employer has forgotten to make provision for this eventuality.

Furthermore, a number of industries and individual companies are exempted from the provisions of the general guarantee payments law because they have a **collective agreement** that provides an alternative scheme of payments. Look in your contract to find out whether your employer has a scheme of guarantee payments.

You may complain to an **employment tribunal** if your employer fails to pay you a guarantee payment, and if you are victimised for making a complaint you are **automatically unfairly dismissed**.

# 6

# Sunday working

The DIY boom of the 1980s and some civil disobedience by large stores saw the demise of Sunday closing. The Sunday Trading Act 1994 allowed shops lawfully to open on a Sunday. Most, but not all, shops now open on Sunday – so the scramble to find one that would sell you mustard under the counter has ended. What protection exists for those who may be obliged to work on a Sunday?

The law allows people to opt out of any normal requirement for Sunday working. However, it does not seem to allow them freely to stipulate from the outset (that is, at their job interview) that they are unwilling to work on a Sunday.

Part IV of the Employment Rights Act 1996 gives special rights with regard to Sunday working for shop and betting workers:

o   There are special provisions relating to work in a shop or work as a betting worker; you may not be required to work on a Sunday (unless, of course, Sunday is the only day upon which you have been employed to work). However, these provisions operate 'in the second case'. You may be taken on in the expectation that you will work on Sundays and you only get the right not to work on a Sunday by filling in a statutory notice saying that you object to Sunday working under s 40 of the Act. In other words, if you go to the interview and say that you do not want to work on Sundays, it seems that the employer has every right not to offer you the job. It is only once you become an employee that you can exercise the right to opt out of Sunday working. This is made clear in s 42 of the Act, where it is provided that an employer has to give the employee a notice within two months of the employee starting work setting out the right to opt out of Sunday working.

o   Furthermore, special provisions apply to workers who were employed before 26 August 1994 for shop workers and 3 January 1995 for betting workers. These workers may not be required to work on a Sunday unless they have given their employer an *opting-in notice* after the relevant date, saying that they:

   –   are willing to work on a Sunday; *and*

   –   have, in fact, worked on a Sunday.

o   Employers are allowed to reduce pay to take account of this refusal to work on a Sunday (ss 36–39).

o   All shop and betting employees have the right to refuse Sunday work, unless they are contracted to work only on Sundays, when a period of three months has elapsed after they have completed an *opting-out notice*, which their employer is required to give them. This notice is in **statutory** form – in other words, the law dictates how it is set out. Of course, your employer is not required to pay you on days on which you do not work (ss 40–43).

Section 45 of the 1996 Act provides that whilst an employer may offer an **opted-out worker** a payment to work on a particular Sunday or Sundays, the employer may not subject the worker to any **detriment** because they have refused to work or have chosen to sign an opting-out certificate. These 'any detriment clauses', which attach to a number of rights, are discussed in Chapter 14, where the consequences for the employer of subjecting you to any detriment are set out.

Furthermore, if you are **dismissed** because you refuse to work on a Sunday, you have the right to compensation following a complaint to an **employment tribunal**. This right is set out in Chapter 14.

# 'Blowing the whistle'

What is meant by 'blowing the whistle'? Here is a practical but rather extreme example (but what a gripping soap opera episode it would make!).

Suppose that you are employed as a theatre nurse in a children's hospital and you find out that one of the surgeons is usually drunk when she operates. Furthermore, it is pointless for you to tell the hospital administration because she is married to the Personnel Officer and having an affair with the Chief Executive.

What should you do? If you confront her she will deny everything and may well persuade her husband (who, you will recall, is the Personnel Officer) to dismiss you. Since he thinks that his wife and the Chief Executive are no more than good friends, as they are both women, he will get backing from the Chief Executive, who wants to keep the affair secret.

Do you go to the authorities, or the press, or do you just keep quiet? What would you do if a child died on the operating table?

This matter was first addressed in the Public Interest Disclosure Act 1998, which started life as a private member's Bill. The provisions of the Act have now been incorporated into the Employment Rights Act 1996.

Part IVA of the 1996 Act generally, and s 103A in particular, provide that a person who is dismissed for making a **protected disclosure** shall be treated as being **automatically unfairly dismissed**.

Section 117(4)(b) of the Act provides that there shall be no limit upon any award of compensation. This law is designed to deal with public interest disclosures or 'whistle-blowing': where an employee discovers serious wrong-doing and *blows the whistle*. The drunken surgeon is a good example.

So, if your employer dismisses you for 'blowing the whistle', you are entitled to compensation.

Of course, not just any old whistle-blowing will do. It has to be a 'qualifying disclosure'. A qualifying disclosure is one which shows that one or more of the following things:

o    has happened;

o    is happening; or

o    is likely to happen.

These things are:

o    a criminal offence;

o    a failure to comply with a legal obligation;

o    a miscarriage of justice;

o    damage to a person's health and safety;

o    some damage to the environment; or

o    that someone is concealing one of these.

Who needs to be told?

o    your employer or someone authorised by your employer;

o    a lawyer for the purposes of obtaining legal advice;

o    (if you are a public employee) a Minister of the Crown; or most importantly

o    one of the people described in the  following list.

Please note: this list is *not* complete; the published list extends to some three closely printed pages and is to be found in the Public Interest Disclosure (Prescribed Persons) Order 1999 (SI 1999/1549). Examples are given for each case.

o    Criminal offences – for example, the Audit Commission would investigate fraud or corruption in local government, or the Charity Commissioners fraud in the operation of a charity.

o    Failure to comply with a legal duty – for example, the Civil Aviation Authority for failure to obey civil aviation legislation.

- Miscarriage of justice – for example, the Chief Executive of the Criminal Cases Review Commission.
- Health and Safety – for example, the Health and Safety Executive.
- Environmental damage – for example, the Environment Agency.

In certain circumstances:

- where the discloser fears that they will suffer in some way if they tell any of the other listed parties;
- where there is no person listed (in the Public Interest Disclosure (Prescribed Persons) Order 1999) for the type of disclosure; or
- they have already made a disclosure to their employer or one of the parties listed above,

any other person may be told – this includes the press.

Are there any other conditions? Yes. A disclosure is only protected if it is made:

- in good faith;
- where the discloser reasonably believes the information disclosed to be true, and that any allegation they have made is substantially true;
- not for the purposes of personal gain,

in other words, if:

- your motives are pure;
- you believe what you say is true; and
- you are not 'on the make'.

So, given the facts we have set out above, you would be protected if you wrote a letter to the Minister of Health drawing their attention to the problem. You would *not* be protected if, instead of writing to the Minister, you sold the story to the *Sunday Shout*, a sensational tabloid newspaper. In this situation you would need to work out whether the payout from the *Sunday Shout* would compensate you for losing your job! Clearly, in the latter case there are lots of issues involving your professional standards and questions of basic morality ... no doubt all of these would be fully explored in the soap opera!

# 8

# Being a good citizen

In some circumstances, you have the right to time off work in order to attend to other duties. These fall into a number of classes. Here we consider those circumstances in which you have the right to be absent from your normal working duties to act as a 'good citizen' – generally as some sort of representative. In succeeding chapters, we will consider other valid reasons for absence from work.

## Health and safety (s 44 of the Employment Rights Act (ERA) 1996)

Sometimes employees are designated by their employer as having special responsibilities for health and safety in the workplace, or they are elected by their workmates (whether or not as members of a trade union) onto a workplace health and safety committee. Clearly this may sometimes annoy the employer because the responsibility is taken rather too seriously for the employer's liking. Employers may not like some danger being drawn to their attention. Thus the Act provides that:

o    if you are designated by your employer as having responsibilities for health and safety at work and you performed those activities; or

o    you are a representative of workers on matters of health and safety and/or you sat on a safety committee; or

o    you took part in **statutory** consultations in the workplace on health and safety; or

- where there is no safety committee in your workplace or it was not practicable for you to ask the committee to raise the matter, you brought your employer's attention by reasonable means to a health and safety problem in the workplace; or

- in a case of reasonably perceived serious and imminent danger which could not be averted you left, proposed to leave or refused to return to your workplace, or you took appropriate steps to protect yourself or others,

you are protected against **detriment** and **dismissal** (see Chapter 14).

## Trusteeship of an occupational pension scheme

Do you remember the Mirror Group pensions scandal in which funds belonging to the employees' pension fund were transferred into the company and many of the employees were left without a pension? The problem was caused in part by the fact that many of the trustees of the scheme were nominees of the late Mr Robert Maxwell and, acting upon the advice which he gave them, they invested heavily in the company. It might have come off, and many of us do put our small amounts of cash into pension and other insurance schemes which do not quite work out as we had planned/hoped/guessed/gambled. The government acted on the report of the inquiry into the failure of the Mirror group scheme and enacted the Pensions Act 1995, which strengthened the role of pensions trustees.

If you are a trustee of an occupational pension scheme you are protected against **detriment** if you act in that capacity. A person who is a trustee of an occupational pension scheme is entitled to paid time off to fulfil that function under ss 58–59 of the ERA 1996 and to complain to an **employment tribunal** if these rights are not granted.

You are protected against **dismissal**.

*Employee representatives* representing workers on a **statutory** representative committee for the purposes of **redundancy** or **transfer of an undertaking** consultation (s 47) are also protected against detriment and dismissal.

To put it more simply, suppose that your employer is planning to make several people redundant, or to transfer the business as a going concern to a new owner. In these circumstances, the workforce is entitled to be consulted. This consultation is done via a committee. If you are a candidate for election to, or a member of, that committee, you are protected from the imposition of a detriment – in other words, you cannot be made to suffer for it. You would be entitled to paid time off to fulfil that function under ss 61–62 ERA 199, and you could complain to an employment tribunal if these rights were not granted.

## Paid time off for young people for study

The law giving a young person the right to paid time off for study (and protection from being victimised for insisting on the right) is to be found in ss 63A, 63B, and 47A of the Employment Rights Act 1996. This law looks untidy because these sections were added to the original Act.

A young person (aged 16–17) who is not in full-time secondary or further education, and who has not attained such a standard of achievement as the Secretary of State lays down in regulations (these include such qualifications as NVQs), is entitled to paid time off to study for a relevant external qualification.

They are not to be subjected to any **detriment** if they seek to exercise that right, provided that it is reasonable with regard to the requirements of the training and the circumstances of, and effect on, the employer's business.

Similarly, a young person aged 18 shall, if they started such training before their 18th birthday, be entitled to complete it. Note that a 'relevant qualification' means one which 'would be likely to enhance the employee's employment prospects (whether with this employer or otherwise)'.

# Public duties

Section 50 of the Employment Rights Act provides that an employee is permitted to take *unpaid, reasonable* time off for the performance of *public duties*.

'Reasonable time off' is assessed by reference to:

o    how much time off is required;

o    how much time off the employee has already been allowed (either for 'public duties' or for 'trade union duties and activities'); and

o    the circumstances of the employer's business and the effect of the employee's absence on the running of that business.

Note: in other words, this is *not* a licence to disrupt your employer's business!

A public duty is defined as:

o    acting as a magistrate;

o    acting as a member of:

–    a local authority;

–    a **statutory tribunal**;

–    a police authority, or the Service Authority for the National Criminal Intelligence Service or the Service Authority for the National Crime Squad;

–    a board of prison visitors or a prison visiting committee;

–    a relevant health body;

–    a relevant education body;

–    the Environment Agency; or

–    a Water and Sewerage Authority or a Water Industry Consultative Committee.

The right is specifically 'to take time off during the employee's working hours for the purposes of a meeting of that body (or its committees or sub-committees) or doing anything approved by the body or for the discharge of any of its functions'.

Much of British public life is rightly undertaken by elected or appointed amateurs who are entitled to time off to fulfil their functions. The problems are:

- ○ whilst some employers recognise the contribution these people make, and allow them to take time off work, the employees have no right to paid time off; and

- ○ whilst many of these bodies do have facilities for members to claim for loss of pay and reasonable expenses, some bodies do not.

This has the effect of restricting the membership to those with sufficiently well-paid jobs to bear the loss of pay that their public duties involve, and of depleting the pool of suitable people available to take on public duties.

If you are denied this right, you may apply to an **employment tribunal** for a declaration that you were entitled to take time off and for compensation for any losses you may have suffered.

*Special provisions apply to members of the Territorial Army and Reserve Forces and you should be given full details of these provisions by your Regiment or Service.*

## Jury service

If you are called for jury service, your employer must give you time off. If this is without pay, you are entitled to some reimbursement from the court. This will not necessarily cover all your costs. When you are called for jury service, you will be sent all the forms you need, together with a useful booklet for guidance – *You and Your Jury Service*. You can find this booklet on the Court Service website at www.courtservice.gov.uk.

# Time off

## Hours and holidays

British workers work some of the longest hours in Europe and there seems to be some sort of machismo/machisma attached to this. The regulation of working time derives from European law and is embodied in the Working Time Regulations 1998.

Here is an outline of the rights provided in the Working Time Regulations. They apply to most workers over compulsory school leaving age:

o a limit of an average of 48 hours per week which a worker can be *required* to work (though workers can *choose* to work more hours if they want to);

o a limit of an average of eight hours in any 24 hours which night workers can be required to work;

o a right for night workers to receive free health assessments;

o a right to 11 hours of rest in a 24-hour day;

o a right to one day off per week;

o a right to an in-work rest break if the working day is longer than six hours;

o a right to four weeks' paid leave per year.

Young workers aged between 15–18 have additional special protections, which we do not discuss in this book – ask the Children's Legal Centre (in 'Useful contacts', p 154) for help.

## Who is *not* protected?

Not all workers are covered by the rights set out in the Working Time Regulations 1998. A number of sectors are excluded from the Regulations. These are:

o    road, rail, air, sea, inland waterway and lake transport;
o    sea fishing;
o    offshore oil and gas work; and
o    the activities of doctors in training.

Everyone agrees, however, that these sectors need their own special rules, and so several new 'horizontal amending directives' amending the parent EC directive are, at the time of writing, coming into force, and the UK government will soon publish fresh regulations. At the time of writing these have not yet been issued.

Other groups who are excluded from the Regulations are:

o    members of the armed forces, police and other civil protection services;

o    ministers of religion;

o    family workers (that is, those working in a family enterprise for family members).

Workers in those sectors which have need for continuity of service (hospitals, prisons, docks, the press, utilities, continuous processing works, etc) have rights in respect of the length of night work, daily and weekly breaks and rest breaks which are slightly modified with respect to the norms set out above.

The other main group of workers who are left out of protection are those who are classed as *autonomous* – that is, they set their own hours of work. Senior managers, freelance writers (like Rosy) and university academics (like Bob) are the most obvious examples.

## Enforcement

Enforcement of the Regulations is split between three bodies. Employees can themselves enforce their entitlements (such as rest periods and breaks and paid annual leave) by taking their case to an **employment**

**tribunal**. In addition, the limits on working time can be enforced by the Health and Safety Executive (HSE), or the local authority can step in to make employers toe the line.

You may not be **dismissed** or subjected to any **detriment** (see Chapter 14) for exercising any of the rights to which you are entitled under the Working Time Regulations 1998. These rights are:

○ to refuse to comply with any requirement in breach of the Working Time Regulations;

○ to 'refuse to forgo' (in other words, to insist on keeping) any right granted by the Regulations;

○ to refuse to sign a workforce agreement varying rights under the Regulations;

○ to stand for election and fulfil the function of a representative provided for in the Regulations;

○ to bring proceedings under the Regulations;

○ to allege that the employer has breached the Regulations.

# 10

# Parents' rights

Parents' rights have always ranked amongst the most complex of **statutory** workers' rights. They were formerly restricted to 'mothers' rights', being linked closely to childbirth, and were based in sex **discrimination** law.

The theory was that employers could not discriminate against mothers because:

o    only women can become mothers; and

o    discrimination against mothers is discrimination against women; and

o    discrimination against women is unlawful.

This theory was challenged on a number of occasions and the law was patched up to block the loopholes. It all became impossibly complicated, so some attempts were made to simplify the law.

However, the law has now widened its scope and working parents are now given many more statutory rights – and some of these statutory rights have been extended to adoptive parents. Please note that these statutory rights are the *minimum* to which you are entitled; it may be that your **contract of employment** contains more generous **contractual** provisions.

Cynics might say that the reason why mothers' rights were made so complex was to discourage mothers from taking them up. This argument may have held force in the early 1990s, but more recently employers too have been complaining about the complexity of the law. This pressure has led to some of the simplification we can see in the Employment Act 2002.

The effect of the Employment Act 2002 has been to make these rights much easier to understand, and the especially good thing about www.tiger.gov.uk (the tailored interactive guidance on employment rights website) is that it contains helpful ready-reckoners to simplify the calculation of entitlement under the new sets of parental rights. All you need to do is connect to www.tiger.gov.uk, select the right which you are interested in, calculate your entitlement, and ensure that you notify your employer. For maternity and paternity leave, this normally means giving 15 weeks' notice.

The cynic might now say that the whole point of making it so easy is to force as many parents as possible to work, and thus reduce the social security budget. The important point to remember is that much of the cost of administering these schemes has now passed to employers, so they have a clear economic incentive for making sure you comply with the long and relatively complex notification arrangements.

The full right to all these different kinds of leave arose on 6 April 2003. Some of the rights existed before that time, so there are transitional arrangements in some cases. Here we set out the basic provisions, but because the rules are tailored to take account of individual circumstances, you should use *tiger* to check your own entitlement in respect of all these rights.

## Maternity leave and pay

In addition to her other maternity rights, a pregnant employee who has been advised to attend ante-natal care has the right to paid time off to do so.

Except for the first such appointment, the employee must show her employer, upon request:

o    a medical certificate stating that she is pregnant; and

o    an appointment card confirming the ante-natal appointment.

This right to attend ante-natal care is provided by ss 55–56 of the Employment Rights Act 1996 and if it is not granted, the employee has the right, by virtue of s 57 of the Act, to complain to an **employment tribunal**.

You become entitled to a full set of **statutory** maternity rights if you satisfy two conditions.

First, you qualify if, by the beginning of the 15th week before your baby is due to be born (that is, 25 weeks into your pregnancy – see below), you have worked for your present employer for 26 weeks.

Given that pregnancy lasts a notional 40 weeks (that's the law – never mind biology!) you need to have worked for 26 weeks before the 25th week of pregnancy. So – some simple advice on how to celebrate getting that new job – make merry by all means, but don't fall pregnant until you have been in your new post for at least a week!

Secondly, you qualify if you earn more than the Lower National Insurance Earnings Limit – currently the lower earnings limit of £75 per week.

The full entitlement to statutory maternity rights includes the following:

o    paid time off for ante-natal care (see above);

o    ordinary maternity leave of 26 weeks provided that you give your employer the proper notification of 15 weeks;

o    additional maternity leave of up to 26 weeks (this starts at the end of your ordinary maternity leave);

o    you must be allowed to go back to the same job when you return to work (in some circumstances your employer may be able to insist that you return to another suitable job);

o    the right not to suffer **detriment** and not to be **dismissed** (see Chapter 14) on grounds related to your pregnancy.

You will get 26 weeks' **statutory maternity pay** (SMP) – SMP is 90% of your salary for the first six weeks and £100 for the remaining 20 weeks – and this is paid by your employer, who reclaims it as a credit from the National Insurance Fund.

For the sake of your own health and safety, you *must* take a period of compulsory maternity leave. This is a short period following the birth of your baby – two weeks if you work in a shop or office, four weeks if you work in a factory. You are obliged to take this leave whether or not you exercise your right to ordinary maternity leave.

When you have completed one year's **continuous employment** you will qualify for parental leave (see below).

While you do not have an enforceable legal right to return to work on a part-time/job-share basis, you do have a right to ask your employer to consider making an alteration to your terms and conditions of employment and, if you do ask to return to work on this basis, your employer must consider your request objectively and genuinely. If they do not consider your request, or if they reject it on 'insubstantial, subjective or unacceptable grounds', you could take an action against them in the employment tribunal for sex discrimination and/or **constructive dismissal**. You can find details of this right on www.tiger.gov.uk under the heading 'flexible working'.

It is important to note that these are *minimum* statutory entitlements. Your **contract of employment** may well carry entitlements to longer periods of maternity leave and higher levels of pay, whether in general or in certain specified circumstances. It may well be that any entitlement to more generous provisions has a longer qualifying service period.

If you do not qualify for these benefits because, for example, you do not have qualifying service, you may qualify for a lower level of benefit.

If you do not qualify for these maternity rights you may qualify for some social security benefit payments. Check out www.tiger.gov.uk to see what you are entitled to.

## Paternity leave

Fathers of children, or husbands or partners of mothers who are expecting a baby, are entitled under the usual service conditions set out above (six months' continuous service, more than £75 per week pay, and normally 15 weeks' notification) to a short period of paternity leave – either one or two weeks according to choice – if:

o    they have responsibility for bringing up the child; and

o    they want to take time off to care for the mother and baby soon after the baby's birth.

The entitlements are as follows:

o    up to two weeks' **statutory** paternity leave (SPL) which can be taken in one block of either one or two weeks. Statutory paternity pay is paid in respect of this leave, and it is either £100 per week or, if you earn less than £100 per week, 90% of your average pay. SPL cannot start before the child has been born and cannot continue later than the 56th day after the date of childbirth or the 56th day after the expected date of childbirth (whichever is the later). You must give your employer the correct notification of (normally) 15 weeks;

o    the right to return to the same job when you go back to work;

o    the right not to suffer unfair **detriment** and not to be **dismissed** or selected for **redundancy** on grounds related to your paternity leave.

This entitlement is the *minimum* statutory entitlement; it may be that your employer grants more generous terms in your **contract of employment**.

When you have completed one year's **continuous employment** you will qualify for parental leave.

## Adoptive leave and 'paternal' adoptive leave

These new rights are based upon the provisions for maternity/paternity leave and pay. The rights are almost identical except in two important respects, namely:

o    the special health and safety protections given to new mothers are not granted to adoptive parents; and

o    you are entitled to choose which partner – regardless of gender – takes adoptive leave (like maternity leave) and which partner takes paternal adoptive leave which, of course, makes sense since neither adoptive parent has actually given birth.

The tiger website at www.tiger.gov.uk gives full details for calculating your entitlements. Be sure that you have your 'matching date' – the date on which you were informed that you had been paired with a child – and the date on which the child will come to live with you.

There is, however, one important exception to the right to adoptive and paternal adoptive leave: *you only gain the right if you adopt a child from within the UK.*

## Time off for children and dependants

The rights set out above attach to the process of actually becoming a parent. However, as any parent can tell you, that's only the beginning. Children have accidents – dried beans are remarkably difficult to remove from nostrils; or the childminder gets 'flu. Even partners get into difficulties from time to time – the worst case on which Bob had to advise was when a distraught employer rang him for advice and said that a particular female employee was absent *again* ... this time because she had to take her partner to the hospital because his penis piercing had gone septic! (Yes, she was entitled to emergency time off – but she was warned about her frequent absences.)

Section 57A of the Employment Rights Act (ERA) 1996 provides that employees are entitled to take a reasonable amount of unpaid time off during their working hours in order to take action which is necessary:

o    to provide assistance when a dependant falls ill, gives birth or is injured or assaulted;

o    to make arrangements to care for a dependant who is ill or injured;

o    because of the death of a dependant;

o    because of the unexpected disruption or termination of arrangements for the care of a dependant; or

o    to deal with an incident involving a child which occurs unexpectedly while the child is at school.

Note that in all of these situations you must tell your employer:

o    the reason for your absence; and

o    how long you expect to be absent

as soon as possible.

## What is a dependant?

In this context, a 'dependant' means:

o    a husband, wife, child or parent;

o    a person who lives in your household (such as a partner, parent, boy/girlfriend or live-in lover) but is not an employee, tenant, lodger or boarder; or

o    (in certain circumstances) any person who reasonably relies on you to make arrangements for the provision of care (for example, the old person next door for whom you cook meals on a regular basis).

If you are denied this right, you may apply to an **employment tribunal** for a declaration that you were entitled to take time off and for compensation for any losses you may have suffered.

## Parental leave

Parental leave was first introduced in December 1999 as a provision of the Employment Relations Act 1999. The idea was to give parents of children born or adopted after December 1999 a right to take a period of time off work. In the recent formulation it is designed to allow parents 'to spend more time with (their) children and strike a better balance between their work and family commitments'. Our cynical commentator might well say – well, that's fine if they can afford to do it because (yes, you've guessed) *the leave is unpaid*. How many people can afford to take time off work with a new baby in the house?

Here is an outline of your entitlements.

Parental leave of 13 weeks for each child (both parents qualify).

The employee has the right to take the leave:

o    until the child's fifth birthday; or

o    until five years have passed following placement in the case of adoption.

(Note that this means 13 weeks over a five-year period, *not* 13 weeks per year.)

Parents of children in receipt of disabled living allowance are able to use their leave over a longer period – up until the child's 18th birthday – and in this case an extra period of five weeks is granted, taking the period of leave to 18 weeks. Such parents are also entitled to take leave in smaller segments.

The employee remains employed while on parental leave; some terms, such as **contractual** notice and **redundancy** terms, still apply.

At the end of parental leave an employee is guaranteed the right to return to the same job as before, or, if that is not practicable, to a similar job which has the same or better status, terms and conditions as the old job. Where the leave taken is for a period of four weeks or less, the employee is entitled to go back to the same job.

Furthermore, there are special transitional arrangements dealing with parents whose children were born before 15 December 1999 (when the right for new parents was introduced), but had not yet reached the age of five by that date.

Once again, www.tiger.gov.uk has full details and a helpful calendar which allows you to plan your parental leave and the necessary notification times.

# Part of the union?

## Your rights to trade union membership – and non-membership

The freedom to exercise trade union membership has been recognised as an essential freedom since the 19th century. It even appears in Article 11 of the European Convention on Human Rights. It is important to recognise that the right is not merely a right to membership, but a right to *exercise* that membership.

You may have heard of the Tolpuddle Martyrs. In 1834, six Dorset farm labourers were tried, convicted and transported. Their names were George and James Loveless, Thomas and John Standfield, James Hammett and James Brine, and they were all being paid nine shillings per week – starvation wages. They decided to set up a union in Tolpuddle to give them some bargaining strength against their employers. The men were challenging the economic power of the Dorset landowners who, led by James Frampton and supported by the government, were determined to suppress any stirrings of rebellion.

But what crime could the men be charged with? Forming a trade union was not a crime. Lord Melbourne provided the answer: administering and taking 'a seditious oath'. This law normally applied to the Navy and had not been applied to trade union activity before, but a trumped-up charge was brought and the Martyrs were found guilty and carted off in chains to the prison hulks. They came home in 1837 after their supporters obtained a free pardon for them.

That having been said, we do not deal in this book with many of the substantive trade union rights afforded to unions themselves, or members and elected officers of trade unions, and we do not deal with trade union democracy at all. We believe that if people wish to be members of trade unions and take part in their activities, it is for the trade unions themselves to inform them of their rights and obligations.

Neither do we tell you about going on strike, because the union has to tell you about that and it has to give you a chance to vote in a secret ballot before calling you out on strike.

Some of these obligations may be duties collectively owed to employers – such as the duty to inform them when the union members are going on strike. Others derive from the general law, especially the Trade Union and Labour Relations (Consolidation) Act 1992 as amended, and some derive from the rule books of the respective unions.

We know where we are with the Act, but as far as the rule books go we are at a loss. Each union has different rules and we cannot advise you about your own union.

Remember, no one can:

o   make you join, not join, remain in membership, or leave a trade union or a particular trade union; or

o   subject you to any **detriment** on the basis of such choices.

Here we deal with:

o   the 'gatehouse' right – to be free from **discrimination** for being or not being a member of a trade union; and

o   the right of individual trade union members to be accompanied by a trade union officer in a disciplinary or grievance hearing.

Here are a number of important 'buzzwords' which apply to this part of employment law.

An *independent trade union* is one which is certified by a special government officer (called the Certification Officer) as free from the control of, or dependence upon, an employer or employers.

The alternative *non-independent* organisation is often known as a 'staff association'. Members of a staff association do not enjoy the **statutory** legal rights granted to trade union members but they may be granted similar **contractual** rights.

A *recognised trade union* is one which has concluded an agreement with the employer that it, and no other trade union without its agreement, may represent members on a particular grade for the purposes of **collective bargaining**. A recognised trade union enjoys certain rights.

The *appropriate time for trade union activity* is defined as 'outside working hours' *or* a time within working hours by arrangement with, or with the consent of, the employer.

Note that some trade unions form themselves into confederations. Moreover, some employers recognise a number of trade unions for the purposes of collective bargaining and these favoured unions often try to exclude other unions from the workplace.

For example, some years ago one of the leading British universities recognised the trade unions AUT (Association of University Teachers), MSF (Manufacturing, Science and Finance), Unison and the TGWU (Transport & General Workers' Union). A union official representing SOGAT (Society of Graphical and Allied Trades) wished to attend to represent a member employed on a grade for which MSF was the recognised union. Since it was neither a disciplinary nor a grievance matter (see p 73), the employer refused to recognise the SOGAT official. The employer could lawfully do so in these circumstances, but could *not* lawfully discipline the employee for being a SOGAT member. Furthermore, the recognised trade unions were very happy to help the employer keep SOGAT out.

Section 137 of the Trade Union and Labour Relations (Consolidation) Act 1992 gives you a right to freedom from **discrimination** on the basis of trade union membership at the point of entry to a job.

It is unlawful to refuse you employment:

○ because you are or are not a member of a trade union; or

o    because you are unwilling to accept a requirement:

  –    to take steps to become, or cease to be, or to remain, or not to become, a member of a trade union;

  –    to make payments (or suffer deductions) if you are not a trade union member,

and, if you are unlawfully refused employment, you have a right to complain to an **employment tribunal**.

Section 146 of the Trade Union and Labour Relations (Consolidation) Act 1992 gives you a right to freedom from action short of dismissal on the basis of your trade union membership or non-membership while you are working in a job.

You have the right not to be subjected to any detriment as an individual by any act, or any deliberate failure to act (such as 'failing to grant' you a pay rise!) by your employer, if the act or failure to act takes place for the purpose of:

o    preventing, deterring or penalising you for being or seeking to become a member of a trade union;

o    preventing, deterring or penalising you for taking part in the activities (such as branch meetings, elections, etc, but not industrial action) of a trade union;

o    compelling you to be or become a member of any trade union or a particular trade union, or one of a number of trade unions.

If the employer takes any such action against you, you have the right to complain to an employment tribunal.

## Employer's defence

In any hearing at a tribunal it is for the employer to show their reason for taking action, because there is a **statutory** defence available to the employer contained in s 148 of the Trade Union and Labour Relations (Consolidation) Act 1992.

We need an example to illustrate it. Suppose that your employer offers you a 10% pay rise if you will make an agreement with them to enter into a new **contract of** employment which will exclude the **collective agreement** on pay, holidays and hours entered into by your employer and the trade union of which you are a member. Your employer does not offer that deal to anyone else.

The question arises as to whether your employer has acted, or in respect of your colleagues, failed to act, for the purpose of deterring you from being a member of that trade union.

This shows the force of our earlier comment about union membership being more than an empty or formal right. The employer says, 'No, I did not want to influence your trade union membership, I just wanted an individual deal with you, different from the one which I offer everyone else'. Would this be caught by s 146? No, it would not be unlawful unless you could show that the employer's action was one which *no reasonable employer* would take.

Sections 152 and 153 provide you with a right not to be dismissed or selected for **redundancy** on the basis of trade union membership or activities.

It is **automatically unfair** for you to be dismissed if the **dismissal** was because you:

o   were or proposed to become a member of an independent trade union;

o   had taken part or proposed to take part at an appropriate time in the activities of an independent trade union;

o   were not a member of any trade union or of a particular union or one of a number of trade unions, or refused or proposed to refuse to become or remain a member.

## Your rights to be accompanied to a disciplinary or grievance hearing

You have a right to have someone with you at any disciplinary or grievance hearing arranged by your employer, and to assert this right by making a complaint to an **employment tribunal**. If you or the person who accompanies you is dismissed as a result of the exercise of this right, it is **automatically unfair**. The right is contained in s 10 of the Employment Relations Act 1999.

The person who accompanies you must be someone of your choice, from the list given below. The meeting may be put back in time to allow your representative to attend.

Your representative must be allowed to address the hearing, but may not answer questions on your behalf.

You and your representative must be allowed to confer – which, in this context, means going into a huddle to discuss things – during the hearing.

The single person who may accompany you must be chosen from:

o   an official employed by a trade union, whether or not the employer recognises the trade union;

o   an official of the trade union (often known as a shop steward or departmental representative) whom the union has certified as having experience of, or has had training in, representing workers; or

o   a colleague.

If you are a trade union member, use your trade union to represent you. You are paying for it.

## More rights

### Special trade union rights to be consulted

If you are a member of a trade union and that union is recognised by the employer, it gains a number of special rights to be consulted about a range of issues. The issues which are of particular concern are those regarding **redundancy**, the sale of a business as a going concern (**transfer of undertaking**) and health and safety. If there is no trade union, these rights devolve to elected representatives of workers. The problem for such non-trade union representatives is that, whilst they may be knowledgeable and highly motivated themselves, they usually lack the detailed and specialist knowledge available to trade unions, who usually pay for the highest quality legal advice. Workers' representatives can, of course, buy in such advice but it can be expensive.

## Recognition

Recognised trade unions have a number of collective rights, and if you (and your workmates) want a trade union to represent you, contact the one which seems right for your sector of employment. For example, widget makers are much more likely to find that Amicus or the Transport & General Workers' Union is more helpful to them than the Fire Brigade Union, the National Union of Miners or the National Union of Teachers. The Trades Union Congress website address, www.tuc.org.uk, will be very happy to help.

A trade union will help you to get your new branch recognised by the employer.

# Discrimination and harassment

You have a legal right to be free from certain kinds of **discrimination** at work. It is misleading to say that you have an unqualified (that is, complete and unconditional) right to be free from discrimination, so we are very careful with our use of words. However, if your employer is a *public body* you are also entitled to enjoy all the rights and freedoms guaranteed by the European Convention on Human Rights without discrimination on any grounds.

Your employer and workmates may not discriminate against you on the grounds of your:

o   race or ethnic origin;

o   sex or transsexualism; or

o   disability.

Furthermore, if, *and only if*, your employer is a public authority, it has further obligations:

o   not to discriminate against you in ways forbidden by the Human Rights Act 1998; *and*

o   to promote racial equality imposed by the Race Relations (Amendment) Act 2000.

Notice that the race and sex discrimination laws require all races and both sexes to be treated as equals. Race or sex conscious treatment is usually unlawful, although there are special health and safety provisions which apply to pregnant or breast-feeding workers.

However, the Disability Discrimination Act 1995 does not provide for equality between disabled and non-disabled persons; an employer may, or in some cases must, make special arrangements for people living with disabilities.

## What are your rights?

Your fundamental rights are:

o   to be treated on your own merits irrespective of your sex (whether or not your sex is the one you were born with) or race with regard to:

– recruitment and selection,

– retention (being kept on the strength),

– access to training, and

– promotion;

o   women and men must be paid equally for work of equal value;

o   if you are living with a disability, you have the right

– to be treated on the basis of what you *can* do rather than what you *cannot* do, and

– to have reasonable adjustments made to premises and work practices to enable you to do the job;

o   to be free from harassment or bullying at work on the basis of your race, sex or disability. This right extends to cover:

– your employer,

– your workmates, and

– anyone else whom you lawfully encounter in your work – for example, customers or contractors;

o   to be free from victimisation if you make a complaint about **discrimination**.

## Direct or indirect discrimination?

There are two basic legal categories of **discrimination**:

o   direct discrimination; and

o   indirect discrimination.

What do these mean?

**Direct discrimination** is said to occur when an employer, or any other discriminator, imposes a rule which explicitly places, for example, women (or men, or black people, or white people) in one position and the corresponding class (respectively, men, women, white people, black people) in another position.

For example, imagine an advertisement 'Workers wanted; no Irish'. This is direct discrimination on the basis of race and is unlawful. No matter what the employer says, he or she may not justify this discrimination; there is no excuse.

**Indirect discrimination** is said to occur when an employer, or any other discriminator, imposes a rule which bears more heavily upon one race or gender, even though the race or gender is not explicitly mentioned. For example, imagine an advertisement 'Workers wanted; must not wear beards'.

This does not mention men, but it clearly impacts more heavily upon men and, furthermore, it impacts more heavily upon, for example, Orthodox Jews (an ethnic group) and Sikhs (another ethnic group). The employer said, in the case from which this example was taken, 'Hang on here, I have absolutely nothing against men, Orthodox Jews or Sikhs, but I am trying to run a chocolate factory and beard nets just do not work as well as hairnets. My customers simply do not want to run the risk of finding hairs from beards in their chocolate'. Indirect discrimination may be justified, as it was in this case, by an employer showing that the restriction imposed is:

o   necessary;

o   appropriate to the perceived problem; and

o   represents the least discriminatory option.

There is an important point here: suppose that there was a requirement for a worker to wear a beard because, for example, the worker was to play the part of a member of the Taleban in a play. Similarly, one could reasonably imagine that:

o   the producer of a play wanted a woman to play the part of Juliet;

o   a gym wanted a woman to run the women-only aerobics classes and supervise the women's changing room;

o   a Chinese restaurant wanted an Asian person as a member of waiting staff;

o   a club wanted a mixed-sex couple to act as 'landlord' and 'landlady'.

All of these cases might well come under the headings of **genuine occupational qualifications** under the provisions of the race and sex discrimination Acts. This is discrimination, but it is lawful.

Let's now have some examples of unlawful discrimination.

These are taken from real life cases.

## Equal pay

Claims for equal pay for women and men are made under the provisions of the Equal Pay Act 1970 or Article 141 of the Treaty of Rome.

There is no equivalent provision relating to pay equality between people of different races.

Senior speech therapists were paid much less than senior pharmacists or senior clinical psychologists, although all three jobs were equally demanding and required equivalent amounts of training and experience. Speech therapists, naturally enough, wanted to be paid on the basis of their skill, qualifications and contribution to health rather than at a lower rate.

It was observed that, perhaps for historical reasons, the majority of speech therapists were women, whilst the majority of clinical psychologists and pharmacists were men. Dr Enderby, the speech therapist who brought the case, succeeded in her claim for pay equality with her male opposite numbers and the NHS was obliged to redesign its job evaluation scheme to ensure pay equality.

However, in a later case a number of women teachers with similar qualifications to a group of more highly paid male teachers failed in their claim for equal pay. Both groups of teachers had similar responsibilities. However, the employer was able to show by way of defence that sex was not a factor in allocating a higher-paid post to a particular teacher.

Equal pay claims are among the most difficult to run successfully. Perhaps this explains why, 30 years after the legislation was first brought into force, women's pay remains on average lower than men's pay. If you are thinking of taking an equal pay claim, seek advice from a specialist solicitor, the Equal Opportunities Commission (see 'Useful contacts', p 153) or your trade union.

## Different jobs or conditions of work for women and men

It is generally unlawful to have different conditions for men and women. Whilst an early case held that allowing women to leave work five minutes earlier than men to avoid getting killed in the rush *did not* amount to unlawful **discrimination**, the case which immediately followed it held that reserving dirty jobs for men *did* amount to unlawful discrimination.

For the employer to insist that only women work on particular jobs, or only people of a certain race work in 'that workshop', is likely to amount to unlawful discrimination. For an employer to insist that women must wear skirts and blouses, whilst allowing men in the same job to wear t-shirts and jeans, is likely to amount to unlawful discrimination. However, if an employer insisted on a *uniform dress code* saying that women must wear dresses or business suits and men must wear suits, collars and ties, the employer is unlikely to be found liable for unlawful discrimination.

Dress codes in general can be tricky because they are obvious sources of discrimination. People do like to wear items of clothing which reflect their ethnic origin – the hijab, the turban and perhaps the kilt are examples. The prudent and sensitive employer would have a clause in their dress code which said something like 'As part of our smartness at work policy headgear may not be worn at work unless it is for *bona fide* religious reasons and complies with the articles of faith'. This would allow, for example, the turban, hijab, patka or yarmulka worn by the devout and exclude the baseball cap worn by Jack the lad (or Jackie the ladette!).

## Shift patterns

In an important case dealing with shift patterns, the courts held that the imposition of a shift pattern which made it very difficult to obtain childcare to cover working hours showed **indirect discrimination** against women. It was held to be indirectly discriminatory because it was acknowledged that while both women and men may have responsibilities for childcare, it was much more likely that the responsibility would fall upon women. However, London Underground, the employer in question, failed to justify the new shift system which they had introduced because it operated as an effective bar to prevent women becoming underground train drivers, and there were no good and sufficient reasons to justify this practice.

## Harassment

Harassment could be defined as 'any words or conduct which create a hostile or offensive working environment and which are offensive or unacceptable to the recipient'.

The latest legal definition talks of 'unwanted conduct that is intended to, or that creates the effect of, violating a person's dignity or that creates an intimidating, hostile, degrading, humiliating or offensive environment for that person', and the various regulations go on to say, 'This definition of harassment will be adopted across other equality areas and is in keeping with the concept that has been developed through **case law**'.

Harassment does not have to be intentional. It may be based on a person's sex, race or disability, but it is not limited to such instances. A one-off act, if it is sufficiently serious and objectively offensive, can amount to harassment.

Employers have a legal duty to take reasonable steps to protect the health and safety of their workers. As well as being alert to obvious risks, employers are obliged to give their workers reasonable support to ensure that they can do their job without being harassed or bullied by fellow workers or others.

'Others' includes visitors to the workplace and also, of course, the employers themselves. For example, for an employer to interfere in a sexual fashion with an employee's clothing or to indecently assault the employee is always sexual **discrimination**. It is also likely to be a criminal offence and should be reported to the police.

There have been a number of cases dealing with indecent or racial assaults upon staff by colleagues. In one case of indecent assault a male supervisor put his hand up a female employee's dress.

In another case, known as *Tower Boot Co v Jones*, two white workers racially abused a black colleague before throwing metal bolts at his head, whipping him with a piece of leather and branding him with a red hot screwdriver.

These are both very serious matters and the courts quickly held that the employers had a **vicarious liability** to pay the victims compensation. In the *Tower Boot* case, the two abusers were successfully prosecuted as well.

What if the assault is 'merely' verbal? We have already mentioned the female employee of a cleaning company who was greeted by the boss's son with the immortal phrase 'Hiya Big Tits'. This is discrimination, because he would not have said it to a man (at least one hopes not!). The complainant, Ms Heads, although her **constructive dismissal** claim failed, succeeded in her claim for discrimination at the **employment tribunal**.

Perhaps the most valuable case in the law of harassment is *Burton and Rhule v De Vere Hotels*. Here the complainants were members of waiting staff at the respondent's hotel in Derby. The dining room was hired out to the local Round Table, who had hired Mr Bernard Manning to provide the after-dinner entertainment. When the two young ladies entered the room while Mr Manning was speaking, he made a number of comments about their sex and race which they found grossly offensive. Indeed it is highly likely that most people, whatever their sex or race, would have found Mr Manning's comments extremely offensive.

Ms Burton and Ms Rhule took proceedings against the hotel – their employer – claiming that their employer should have protected them from Mr Manning's offensive speech. They succeeded. This case seems to indicate that, where employers know that their staff may be subjected to talk that is discriminatory, they have a duty to protect them from it.

Many employers spend a great deal of time and effort in trying to keep their workplaces free from harassment and bullying, and have specially trained confidential harassment advisers on their staff. If your employer provides this service, do make use of it. Very often it can resolve problems which fall short of the legal definition of unlawful **discrimination** but which are, nonetheless, making your working life miserable.

In some circumstances, harassment may amount to a criminal offence; however, there is a difference between the level of evidence needed for establishing *civil* liability (typically in a county court, here in the **employment tribunal**) and that needed to establish *criminal* liability (in a criminal court). Do not attempt to activate the 'criminal route' until you have taken legal advice and unless the problem is very serious.

Needless to say, if you are subjected to a criminal assault at work, such as the one experienced by Mr Jones in the *Tower Boot* case, or you are indecently assaulted, you should go to the police *immediately*.

## Gender reassignment or transsexualism

Clearly **gender reassignment** or 'changing sex' is a big step for anyone to take. Unfortunately, some employers, perhaps under pressure from employees, do not like it and discriminate against people who undertake the treatment.

In the most famous case, P, a librarian, was dismissed by her employer, Cornwall County Council, when, having obtained and worked in the job for some time as a man, she underwent surgery and hormone treatment and became a woman. Her supervisor in the library service took exception to this and dismissed her. P claimed at the Bodmin **employment tribunal** that she had suffered **discrimination**. The tribunal took the bold but entirely justified step of sending the matter to the European

Court of Justice (ECJ). The ECJ held that the Equal Treatment Directive, which requires the equal treatment of women and men, also requires the equal treatment of transsexuals – and P won her case.

## Disability discrimination

An employer has a legal duty to make reasonable adjustments to working practices in order to allow a disabled person to do the job. A number of cases will help to demonstrate the central features of the law.

In *Tarling v Wisdom Toothbrushes* the employer was held to have discriminated against Mr Tarling when it failed to provide him with seating to allow him to do his job. Mr Tarling suffered from a life-long deformity of his foot and found it difficult to sit or stand for long periods.

In *Kenny v Hampshire Constabulary*, Mr Kenny, who had cerebral palsy, applied for a job as a civilian worker for Hampshire Police. The Service tried to make reasonable arrangements to help him to do the job, even to the extent of providing him with a helper. All these efforts failed and the Service withdrew the job offer. Mr Kenny failed in his action for unlawful **discrimination**, the tribunal holding that the employer had taken all reasonable steps to accommodate his requirements.

Finally, in *O'Neill v Symm & Co*, the employer was held not to have discriminated against Ms O'Neill when she misled them about the disease from which she was suffering. They could not have discovered the true nature of the disease because of her frequent absences from work. The tribunal held that Ms O'Neill was dismissed because of her absence rather than her disability. A disabled employee is under an obligation to bring the disability to the attention of his or her employer so that the employer may make reasonable accommodation for the disability.

### What should employees do if they are subjected to unlawful discrimination?

It is quite clear that employees have an obligation to bring the matter to their employer's attention. It is for the employer to deal with the complaint in the first instance. If the employer fails properly so to do, the employer is liable. Furthermore, if the employer victimises the employee for complaining, this is itself a civil wrong (the lawyers' word is *tort*) and the employer is liable to pay compensation.

## What should employees do if the employer fails to take action?

A number of agencies may be willing to give you free legal assistance and support in your claim:

o the Equal Opportunities Commission (gender and sex discrimination);

o the Commission for Racial Equality (race discrimination);

o the Disability Rights Commission (disability rights).

See 'Useful contacts', pp 153–54, for their details.

Furthermore, these agencies do have, in extreme cases, the power to undertake formal investigations into organisations who are reasonably thought to be practising widespread or institutional **discrimination**.

For example, the Equal Opportunities Commission undertook an investigation into the airline Dan Air, who refused to employ men as cabin staff on the stated grounds that 'men who wanted to be cabin staff were often homosexuals who might catch AIDS'!

The agencies see their job as trying to help by providing assistance and persuasion rather than by coercion. They are very happy to give informal advice and help to organisations who want to avoid discrimination but are unsure of their way through the legal and social minefield.

You could also go to your trade union for help in your workplace, or to the local Citizens Advice Bureau (CAB) or law centre, or to a solicitor for legal help.

# 13

# Health and safety rights

The core legal right is contained in s 2 of the Health and Safety at Work etc Act 1974. We reproduce the entire section below because, whilst its language is slightly opaque, it makes your rights clear. We have put some of the key words into **bold italic** type. We explain some of these concepts and comment upon them below.

By the way, *he/his* includes *she/her*.

(1) It shall be the duty of every employer to ensure, *so far as is reasonably practicable*, the health, safety and welfare at work of all his employees.

(2) Without prejudice to the generality of an employer's duty under the preceding subsection, the matters to which that duty extends include in particular –

(a) the *provision and maintenance* of plant and systems of work that are, so far as is reasonably practicable, safe and without risks to health;

(b) *arrangements* for ensuring, so far as is reasonably practicable, safety and absence of risks to health in connection with the use, handling, storage and transport of articles and substances;

(c) *the provision of such information, instruction, training and supervision* as is necessary to ensure, so far as is reasonably practicable, the health and safety at work of his employees;

(d) so far as is reasonably practicable as regards any place of work under the employer's control, the maintenance of it in a condition that is safe and without risks to health and the provision and maintenance of means of access to and egress from it that are safe and without such risks;

(e) the provision and maintenance of a working environment for his employees that is, so far as is reasonably practicable, safe, without risks to health, and adequate as regards facilities and arrangements for their welfare at work.

(3) Except in such cases as may be prescribed, *it shall be the duty of every employer to prepare and as often as may be appropriate revise a written statement of his general policy with respect to the health and safety at work of his employees and the organisation and arrangements for the time being in force for carrying out that policy*, and to bring the statement and any revision of it to the notice of all his employees.

(4) Regulations made by the Secretary of State may provide for the appointment in prescribed cases by recognised trade unions (within the meaning of the regulations) of *safety representatives from amongst the employees*, and those representatives shall represent the employees in consultations with the employers under subsection (6) below and shall have such other functions as may be prescribed.

[There is no section 5 now – it was repealed in 1978 and the numbering was never amended.]

(6) It shall be the duty of every employer to consult any such representatives with a view to the making and maintenance of arrangements which will enable him and his employees to co-operate effectively in promoting and developing measures to ensure the health and safety at work of the employees, and in checking the effectiveness of such measures.

(7) In such cases as may be prescribed it shall be the duty of every employer, if requested to do so by the safety representatives mentioned in [subsection (4)] above, to establish, in accordance with regulations made by the Secretary of State, *a safety committee* having the function of keeping under review the measures taken to ensure the health and safety at work of his employees and such other functions as may be prescribed.

So, to put it all in a more user-friendly way you have the right to expect your employer to give you, *as far as is reasonably practicable*:

o   a safe and healthy workplace;

o   safe systems of work;

o   information about the hazards you might face;

o   training to allow you to cope with the hazards at work;

o   (in organisations with more than five employees) a written statement of Health and Safety Policy;

o   a statement of how safe working practices are to be achieved.

Normally this would mean telling you about the works safety officer, who has special responsibilities for health and safety, and how to raise health and safety issues at work. This also includes, under a variety of regulations, the obligation to carry out formal **risk assessments**.

If you and your colleagues, in a trade union or otherwise, want your employer to form a Safety Committee, they must provide you with one. They must, in any event, consult you about health and safety issues.

Furthermore, there is a **statutory** poster dealing with health and safety matters which the employer *must* display. If you have not seen it in the workplace, do go and look for it!

The key phrase in the law, which *may* limit your rights, is *so far as is reasonably practicable*. This means that your employer does *not* have an open-ended duty to comply with all requests on health and safety issues, nor do they have a duty to guard against all possible risks, or at least, that is the situation in most cases. The **case law** is complicated, not least because it contains a mixture of civil law (the law of personal injury, enforced in the civil courts), criminal law (employers are prosecuted for serious breaches of health and safety legislation) and 'regulatory law'.

We mean by 'regulatory law', those substantive standards of health and safety which are contained, usually in regulations (statutory instruments), which may derive either from European or from English sources. These standards may, alternatively, be contained in 'AcoPs' (or Approved Codes of Practice) which are issued by the Health and Safety Executive as constituting 'good practice' when dealing with a particular hazard. These are sometimes, somewhat disparagingly, called 'leaflet law' or (worse still) 'glossy pamphlet law' by lawyers. An AcoP has, of itself, no legal force but it is to be taken into account when construing the law. What is more, the law has been developed in response to actual injuries at work.

## So what?

What principles can we see at work here? First, it would seem that an employer has the duty to carry out a **risk assessment** of any work or process which is taking place. The employer is under a duty to listen to representations about that process from employees.

If you have any concerns about health and safety in the workplace, raise them with:

o    the safety committee; or

o    your employer.

You have a right *not* to be subjected to any **detriment** or **dismissal** (that is, not to be victimised or sacked) for so doing.

The employers must place themselves in a position to show that, weighing the risk to health against the means, including the cost, of eliminating the risk, it was not reasonably practicable for them to take measures to eliminate the risk. This seems to indicate that the duty is *qualified* by what is practicable and reasonable. However, some of the **case law** seems to show that the duty is *absolute* – employers *must* eliminate risks to health and safety. This seems to arise in two sorts of cases:

o    where the risk is obvious or the consequences are so severe (death or serious injury); *or*

o    there is a special **statutory** regime in the situation under discussion that provides for a standard of absolute liability.

We need to be cautious in giving examples, because it is very difficult to generalise from specific examples. The first case of an obvious serious injury might be illustrated by a case in which a machine fitter injured his arm.

A machine fitter was employed in a factory where there was a large conveyor belt suspended on heavy rollers. He was asked to repair the conveyor and one of the rollers slipped and crushed his arm. *The company was held liable because the risk was so obvious to them that they ought to have carried out a formal risk assessment and used special safety measures.*

The second case is illustrated by that of a postman who was thrown over the handlebars of his bike and was seriously injured when a brake fitting snapped. *The Post Office was held to have an absolute liability to him to ensure that he had safe working equipment.*

Do interpret these examples with extreme caution, as a great deal depends on the regulatory regime in the circumstances. By 'regulatory regime' we refer to the fact that in different industries, using different machines and processes, different rules apply. This is common sense – no one would want the rules which apply in, say, a nuclear power plant to apply in, say, a nursery (children or plants!).

A recognised trade union has a right to be consulted over matters of health and safety and there is a procedure, well known to trade unions, whereby this consultation process can be activated.

If you are a trade unionist, contact your union about your rights in this matter.

Furthermore, in workplaces where there is no recognised trade union, the employees – *unless the employer says that employees will be consulted directly* – have a right to elect representatives so that proper consultations with the employer can take place. The rights are set out in the Health and Safety (Consultation with Employees) Regulations 1996 (SI 1996/1513).

1   If there is a group of workers at your workplace and you feel that you are not being properly consulted, get hold of the Regulations and approach your employer. Remember that the employer is under a legal duty to consult, so that simply saying 'Employees will be consulted directly' and then doing nothing about it will simply not do.

2   If you try to talk to your employer about health and safety matters and are subjected to a **detriment** (victimised) or you are **dismissed**, you have a right to take a complaint to an **employment tribunal**.

## Risk assessments

**Risk assessments** are key issues in modern health and safety law. They are the means by which your employer should assess the risks you face at work. All employers are required to *perform* these risk assessments, but they are only obliged to *record* the assessments if they employ more than five people.

Employers are obliged to carry out risk assessments under a number of specific health and safety Regulations. For example, under regulation 4(1) of the Manual Handling Operations Regulations 1992 (SI 1992/2793), employers must:

(a)   so far as is reasonably practicable, avoid the need for their employees to undertake any manual handling operations at work which involve a risk of their being injured; or

(b)   where it is not reasonably practicable to avoid the need for their employees to undertake any manual handling operations at work which involve a risk of their being injured:

(i)   Make a suitable and sufficient assessment of all such manual handling operations to be undertaken by them, having regard to the factors ... and considering the questions ... [which are listed in the appropriate legislation and need not detain us here].

## Mothers' rights

Pregnant women and nursing mothers are entitled to special protection under the English regulatory scheme implementing 'the EC Council Directive (98/85/EEC) on the introduction of measures to encourage improvements in the safety and health of pregnant workers and workers who have recently given birth or are breastfeeding' (phew!). This involves a special **risk assessment** to take account of their own health requirements and those of their babies.

## Young workers

Workers under the age of 18 years similarly have extended protection. Section 3 of the Management of Health and Safety at Work Regulations 1999 (SI 1999/3242) provides that:

(4)  An employer shall not employ a young person unless he has, in relation to risks to the health and safety of young persons, made or reviewed an assessment in accordance with paragraph(s) ... (5).

(5)  In making or reviewing the assessment, an employer who employs or is to employ a young person shall take particular account of –
   (a)  the inexperience, lack of awareness of risks and immaturity of young persons;
   (b)  the fitting-out and layout of the workplace and the workstation;
   (c)  the nature, degree and duration of exposure to physical, biological and chemical agents;
   (d)  the form, range, and use of work equipment and the way in which it is handled;
   (e)  the organisation of processes and activities;
   (f)  the extent of the health and safety training provided or to be provided to young persons; and
   (g)  risks from agents, processes and work listed ...

## What are your obligations?

Your key obligation is to co-operate with your employer in the performance of their legal duty to maintain a safe and healthy working environment. The duties are well set out in ss 7 and 8 of the Health and Safety at Work etc Act 1974:

(7) It shall be the duty of every employee while at work:

(a) to take reasonable care for the health and safety of himself and of other persons who may be affected by his acts or omissions at work; and

(b) as regards any duty or requirement imposed on his employer or any other person by or under any of the relevant statutory provisions, to co-operate with him so far as is necessary to enable that duty or requirement to be performed or complied with.

(8) No person shall intentionally or recklessly interfere with or misuse anything provided in the interests of health, safety or welfare in pursuance of any of the relevant statutory provisions.

We can provide a useful and salutary example of this duty. Employers may be subject to criminal penalties if they allow certain machinery to be operated without a guard. Clearly, prudent employers tell their employees not to remove guards. Nonetheless, one of Bob's former workmates, a man called Joe, disobeyed orders and removed a machine guard in order to perform some work. Joe sawed off the top of his finger!

The employer was prosecuted for allowing the machine to be operated without a guard, and Joe was prosecuted for using the machine without a guard. Bob was the trade union representative in the workplace and subsequently had to defend Joe when the employer tried to sack him for landing the firm in court. Fortunately, the boss realised that Joe had suffered enough and let him stay on.

Comply with your employer's health and safety rules. If you don't, you could be prosecuted or *fairly* **dismissed**.

This book stresses that working is all about using rights within a relationship. The major statute on health and safety – the Health and Safety etc at Work Act 1974 – was the brain child of the Robens Commission.

This was set up in the early 1970s under the chairmanship of Lord (Alf) Robens who came from the National Coal Board (NCB) to enquire into the state and organisation of industrial health and safety. Lord Robens, during his time at the NCB, had modernised and improved the health and safety framework in the mining industry. Whilst coal mining always was an inherently dangerous industry, the co-operative system for maintaining and improving safety had first been introduced in the mining industry during the mid-19th century. Lord Robens brought the system up to date to ensure that workers, unions and management were all equally involved in safety issues. Lord Robens sought, in the Act, to extend this partnership approach to all areas of health and safety management.

## Where should I go for detailed information about health and safety law?

We cannot fit into a book of this size all the detailed information about health and safety law that is now available. The Health and Safety Executive website at www.hse.gov.uk is the best place to start.

# Your right to claim your rights

In the last few chapters we have listed the various rights that the law gives to you. This chapter deals with claiming those rights.

The first person to approach if you have a legal right to something is, of course, your employer. He knows all about rights and responsibilities. After all, he expects his suppliers to keep him supplied and he expects to pay for this service. He expects his customers to pay for goods, and he expects to deliver the goods to the customer.

Similarly, your employer has responsibilities towards the staff, just as you have responsibilities towards your employer. Life is made up of rights and duties. So, after checking carefully that you are entitled to the right you wish to claim, approach your employer, giving him the proper notice and being entirely pleasant and reasonable: as Teddy Roosevelt said, 'speaking softly and carrying a big stick'.

If your employer refuses to grant you your right you can then complain to an **employment tribunal**. Section 48 and some of the following sections of the Employment Rights Act 1996 (depending upon the precise nature of the right that has been infringed) give you the right to complain. The tribunal will, if it finds your complaint well-founded, make a statement of your rights (called a declaration) and will award you compensation for any losses you have suffered.

You might now say, 'Surely if I bring an action against my employer for denying me my **statutory** rights, the first thing my employer is going to do is sack or otherwise punish me! What's the use of that? I won't get my rights and I won't have a job any more!', and then you will complain that we have led you into a minefield.

Wrong! Part V of the Employment Rights Act 1996 gives you the right not to 'suffer **detriment**' in employment if you are engaged in certain activities or choose to exercise your rights at work, *so* if your employer 'subjects you to a detriment' (that is, victimises you) either for asking for a particular right, or for complaining that you have been denied that right, or especially if you are dismissed, you are entitled to complain to the employment tribunal.

In this context, detriment is an ordinary English word and must be given its everyday meaning of 'disadvantage', 'damage' or 'harm'. The opposite would be *advantage*. If you are, for example:

o   refused promotion or downgraded;

o   repeatedly selected for unpleasant work;

o   threatened with the sack if you continue exercising your rights; or

o   dismissed,

you have been subjected to a detriment. We discuss **dismissal** below.

The concept of detriment operates in two important ways.

o   If you are subjected to a detriment for exercising one of your statutory rights as set out above, you have a specific right to bring proceedings in the employment tribunal.

o   If the detriment is so severe that it shows that the employer is simply breaking your **contract of employment**, you have a right to leave, and claim **constructive dismissal**.

## Dismissal for claiming a right

Here we deal with the question of being **dismissed** for claiming a *statutory* right. These rights are set out in Chapters 5–13. Any employer who dismisses you for claiming a statutory right connected with:

- pregnancy or maternity;
- maternity/paternity or adoptive leave;
- health and safety at work;
- refusal to work on a Sunday *if* you are a **protected shop or betting worker**;
- claiming your rights under the Working Time legislation;
- acting as a trustee of an occupational pension scheme;
- making a **protected disclosure** ('blowing the whistle');
- claiming the national minimum wage;
- claiming a tax credit;
- claiming one of the other statutory rights;

*or* who

- infringes one of your trade union rights as set out in Chapter 11;
- infringes one of the health and safety rights as set out in Chapter 13; or
- dismisses you in breach of the minimum standards of fairness in the statutory disciplinary procedure as set out in Chapter 16,

is running a grave risk of being held liable for **unfairly dismissing** you. Such a **dismissal**, if the tribunal holds that it was done for one of these specially protected reasons, is said to be **automatically unfair** and it may be that you are entitled to an enhanced level of compensation.

To be fair, it is only rarely that an employer will do such a (frankly, stupid) thing. Big, well organised and well-advised employers do such things very rarely indeed because their solicitors, legal and personnel departments advise them not to do so; or, if they proceed nonetheless, they are doing it having prepared the ground. They know that they are 'skating on very thin ice' and are doing it:

- to challenge the law;
- because they think they have found a gap in your defence; or
- because they have got a very good reason for wanting to do it.

The most famous case in this area is *Payne v Port of London Authority* which involved the sacking of a number of dock workers for trade union reasons (or so the dockers said; the employers claimed that the dockers were doing things other than engaging in genuine trade unionism). All this took place in the context of the deregulation of dock labour. The employers were trying to make radical changes to the workplace and did not care how much it cost to get their own way. Bob went to watch the **employment tribunal** in this case. There, in front of the allegedly informal, non-legalistic tribunal, leading counsel for the employers was cross-examining the General Secretary of the biggest trade union in Britain. By the time Bob got to watch the proceedings, the two sides had been slugging it out for three months. This was a test case in every sense: the employers were testing the law and everyone knew it. An important **precedent** was going to come out of this case, so both sides wheeled in their heaviest artillery.

The point of this story is that if a big, wealthy, well-advised employer sacks you for something that seems like an **automatically unfair reason**, they are trying it on – just like the Port of London Authority – and you must carefully consider getting professional legal help.

Small employers sometimes step out of line in ignorance and give you a bit more warning. One of the things you could reasonably do is to refer them to the companion volume in this series, *The Employer's Handbook*, which is designed for employers. It could save your employer a great deal of time and money, avoid the employment tribunal and help you keep your job with the rights to which you are legally entitled.

# PART 3
# DISMISSAL AND REDUNDANCY

# Parting company – an outline

## Resignation

The most obvious way of bringing an employment relationship to an end is simply to **resign**, giving your **contractual** notice. There are no restrictions upon your doing this unless you have a very strange employment contract – are you employed as the manager of a football team, or were you taken on to do a particular job, such as providing the lighting for a play? If not, then you can simply resign.

Sometimes things can be a bit more difficult. Your employer may *want* you to leave.

## Sometimes a working relationship goes wrong

The commonest situation in which this takes place is where the employer or senior manager believes that the employee in question cannot do the job and has lost the confidence of colleagues.

Some employers try to use **redundancy** in these situations, but, as we shall see, this is fraught with difficulties.

Other employers simply pitch into the disciplinary procedure and hope that they have got sufficient evidence to dismiss the employee. This often fails because the employee is not performing sufficiently poorly to justify **dismissal**, and the employer becomes jumpy and makes a mistake; then the employee becomes entitled to claim for **constructive dismissal** because the employer has breached the obligation to maintain mutual trust and confidence.

Looked at coolly, the problem is that the working relationship really has failed and it has to be brought to an end for the good of all the parties. In real life, the employee detests the employer and the employer often takes the view that, whilst the employee is a perfectly nice person, they are not doing what the employer really wants.

How should the employee deal with this problem? The only answer is to sit tight and hope that the employer will take the professional way out of the situation. A professional employer will approach an employee, point out that the working relationship is simply not working and ask the employee to *resign*. In consideration of a voluntary **resignation**, the employer will pay a sum of money and in return will ask for an agreement not to pursue the matter in an **employment tribunal**.

Although one cannot normally exclude the jurisdiction of a court or tribunal, it is possible to agree not to take a claim of **unfair dismissal** to a tribunal under the procedure set down in s 203(2)(f) of the Employment Rights Act 1996. This requires the employee to take independent legal advice from a solicitor or other person qualified under the rules set out in subsections (3), (3A) and (3B), or to involve **ACAS** (the Advisory, Concilliation and Arbitration Service).

The usual way of arriving at an agreement is for the employer to have a document drawn up covering the main terms of that agreement, and to offer to pay a solicitor's fees for the employee to receive independent legal advice. The sums of money typically involved are of the order of six months' to one year's pay as a severance payment, inclusive of redundancy pay, holiday pay, etc, and up to £250 + VAT for legal advice. Employers may be willing to pay more where the employee is nearing retirement age and it is possible to negotiate an early retirement package. Commonly, this enables the employer to phase the payments into the employee's pension fund.

If you can, get a solicitor of your own, or a trade union officer (if you are a member) to help you with these negotiations. A third party is often better able to negotiate on your behalf.

If things have gone really sour, the employer may decide to move to bring the employment relationship to an end. This can be for one of two basic reasons:

o    first, for a reason to do with the particular person concerned (that is, you); because, for example, your employer thinks that you can no longer do the job, or that your behaviour is intolerable to the employer;

o    secondly, for a reason which attaches to the firm; for example, it can no longer afford to pay you.

The first kind of dismissal is normally called simply that – dismissal; the second sort is called redundancy.

Let's look at the law.

Part IX of the Employment Rights Act (ERA) 1996 is the first Part of the Act that deals with **termination** of the employment relationship.

Section 86 of the ERA 1996 provides for the rights of an employer and an employee to a *minimum notice period*. We have discussed these rights in our section on the contract of employment (see Chapter 3).

Do remember that the periods of notice set out in s 86 are the *minimum* **statutory** periods of notice. Your **contract of employment** may provide for longer periods of notice on either side. If you leave your employment without giving your **contractual** notice your employer could sue you for loss.

Sections 87, 88 and 89 provide that if, during a notice period:

o    you are ready and willing to work, but your employer fails to provide you with work;

o    you are incapable of work because you are ill or injured;

o    you are absent because you are pregnant or have just given birth or are taking parental leave; or

o    you are on contractual holiday, you are entitled to be paid. There are certain restrictions to this right, notably that you are not entitled to be paid if you are absent from work on trade union duties or for any of the reasons set out in Part VI of the Act (fulfilling public duties, etc). You are entitled to have time off, but not to be paid (see p 55).

Provided that you have been **continuously employed** for one year, s 91 gives you:

o   a right to a written statement of the reasons for your dismissal; and

o   a right to complain to an employment tribunal if, and only if, you decide to claim for unfair dismissal.

## Unfair dismissal

Sometimes an employer messes up a **dismissal** – gets the paperwork wrong, misjudges the notice period or whatever. This may amount to **unfair dismissal** (or **wrongful dismissal** or even **constructive dismissal**) (if you are unsure which is which, see 'Buzzwords', p xv).

The legislation that deals with unfair dismissal is Part X of the ERA 1996. Section 94 ERA 1996 provides that:

o   an employee has the right not to be unfairly dismissed by their employer;

o   subsection (1) has effect – subject to ss 108–10 of the Employment Rights Act 1996 and the provisions of the Trade Union and Labour Relations (Consolidation) Act 1992 (in particular ss 237–39).

We discuss this right in detail in Chapter 16. Notice that the right has certain qualifications attached to it. If you would like a clearer statement of your rights, try this:

A **qualified employee** who has been dismissed has the right to make a timely complaint of unfair dismissal to an **employment tribunal** provided that he or she was not dismissed for being on unofficial strike.

Unfair dismissal is not an everyday phrase, but has a special meaning provided by the **statute** which has been, in turn, developed and explained by the courts.

# Redundancy

Redundancy comes under Part XI of the ERA 1996. Redundancy is a special case of a **potentially fair dismissal**. If your employer makes you **redundant** in a lawful way, you are *fairly* dismissed, but your employer still has to pay you some compensation. This compensation may be **statutory** (the legal minimum) or it may be **contractual** – paid at an enhanced rate set out in your **contract of employment** or otherwise agreed between you and your employer.

If your employer fails to follow the legal rules in making you **redundant**, you are in fact **unfairly dismissed** and you may take a complaint to the **employment tribunal**.

You have *individual rights* in redundancy, but since redundancies often affect a number of workers at the same time, you may also have *collective rights*.

The basic right, analogous to the right not to be **unfairly dismissed**, is to be found in s 135 of the ERA 1996:

(1) An employer shall pay a redundancy payment to any employee of his if the employee –
   (a) is dismissed by the employer by reason of redundancy, *or*
   (b) is eligible for a redundancy payment by reason of being laid off or kept on short time.

(2) Subsection (1) has effect subject to the following provisions of this Part (including, in particular, sections 140–44, 149–52, 155–61 and 164)

and provided that:

o you have been **continuously employed** for a period of two years; *and*

o are not over retirement age; *and*

o have not agreed to exclude your right to a redundancy payment.

There are two other situations that we need to mention now (we will discuss them at greater length below) – **constructive dismissal** (a special case of unfair dismissal) and **wrongful dismissal** (a **dismissal** in breach of contract, useful in circumstances where you do not have the right not to be unfairly dismissed).

# 16

# Unfair dismissal

One of the most important rights in employment law is the right of a **qualified employee** not to be **unfairly dismissed**.

You also need to compare **unfair dismissal** with **wrongful dismissal** and **constructive dismissal** (these are discussed in Chapter 18).

## Who has the right not to be unfairly dismissed?

First, this right is limited to *employees*. That means somebody who is employed under a **contract of service** rather than a **contract for services** (see Chapter 2).

When *The Times* dropped their cookery columnist, she tried to make a claim against them. Her claim failed, not because she had not been treated shabbily but because she was not an employee and therefore did not have the rights which an employee would have. (Are you there, Frances Bissell? Rosy still uses your cook book every day and misses your column *very much*.)

Secondly, it is limited to **qualified employees**. If you have been **continuously employed** by your employer for more than 12 months, you are qualified to bring a claim for **unfair dismissal** *unless* you are:

o    older than the normal retiring age set by your firm; or

o    over 65.

However, there are some cases in which you are qualified to bring an action for unfair dismissal either immediately upon being employed, that is, from your very first day at work, *or* from the time at which you qualify for the right in question (paternity leave rights, etc). The question of **automatically unfair dismissal** is set out in Chapter 14.

## Time limit

Thirdly, you must remember that no matter what else happens you *must* ensure that your claim for **unfair dismissal** reaches the **employment tribunal** office *before three months have elapsed from your date of dismissal*. Your date of dismissal is whichever is the later of the date upon which your notice expired or the day on which you last actually worked. If you are late, even by one day, the tribunal may refuse to hear your claim. The exceptions to this strict rule are so rare as to require no serious treatment. This rule applies to all cases of unfair dismissal.

Mark the vital dates in your diary, with a reminder to yourself, say, a fortnight before any claim is due to be lodged.

Although it is possible to take a claim to an **employment tribunal** yourself, you may wish to take professional legal advice.

You then have to appreciate that the words 'fair' and 'unfair' when applied to a **dismissal** are *not* just everyday words – they have special meanings. When you are dismissed it almost always *feels* unfair, but it may be legally fair. It is even possible that a dismissal which feels fair is legally unfair.

In order to be legally fair the dismissal has to be for a legally permitted reason – known as a **potentially fair reason for dismissal**. In other words, it cannot be for an **automatically unfair reason** or a dismissal for any old reason; it has to be for one of the five legally permitted reasons. Furthermore, the dismissal has to be an appropriate sanction delivered in response to your fault or other reason, and the sanction has to be arrived at in a fair way.

## Potentially fair reasons for dismissal

Remember that when the concept of **potentially fair reasons for dismissal** was introduced in 'Buzzwords', it was pointed out that there are five potentially fair reasons for dismissal. These are contained in s 98 of the Employment Rights Act (ERA) 1996 and are:

o   capability (s 98(2)(a), s 98(3));

o   conduct (s 98(2)(b));

o   **redundancy** (s 98(2)(c));

o   breach of **statutory** provision (s 98(2)(d)); and

o   some other substantially fair reason (s 98(1)(b)).

It is now time to explain what these mean and to set out your rights as a general rule.

### Capability

Imagine that you fall ill and can no longer do your job.

Or imagine that you were originally employed as, for example, a trainee accounts technician on the understanding that you would be employed as a technician when you passed your examinations. Sadly, you have failed the exams four times. In both these circumstances your employer has a **potentially fair reason** for dismissing you.

### Conduct

Clearly, committing theft or criminal damage at work, or failing to do something you have been lawfully asked to do, might constitute a fair reason for **dismissal**. Modern examples of misconduct might well be abuse of the internet (looking at pornographic websites at work) or sending abusive e-mails, or deleting important computer files. Even repeated minor offences might amount to a fair reason, if a proper procedure is followed and proper warnings are given.

## Redundancy

The rules for redundancy have been drawn up very tightly. They are contained in s 139(1) of the ERA 1996. For an employee to be **redundant**:

o    the employer must have ceased, or intend to cease, to carry on the business completely, or in the place where the employee was employed; *or*

o    the business must have discontinued or reduced the amount of the work which the employee was employed to do.

To give a simple example: suppose that the employer decides to stop making typewriters because no one buys them any longer. Specialist typewriter builders are redundant, even though the company may continue to build computers, word processors and electronic tills.

## Breach of statutory provision

Suppose that you are a van driver and you lose your driving licence, or you are a professional huntsman and the government makes hunting illegal. It would be unlawful for you to continue in work.

## Some other substantial reason

This case has been developed by the courts to contain a number of categories of **dismissal**. Some **precedents** which have been set down in the past include the following situations:

o    The activities of an employee at work make him or her totally unacceptable to other employees or customers and the employee's activity is not protected by law.

The most bizarre case, fully worthy of the lurid tabloid press, concerned one Ms Treganowan, whose continual boasting about her sexual exploits so annoyed her fellow workers that her employer felt that he had no alternative but to dismiss her. Her **dismissal** was held to be fair. An exceptionally smelly member of staff might elicit such a response.

- Customers force a dismissal, as in the cases of *Dobie v Burns International Security*, who was sacked because a customer would not allow him onto their premises, and *Saunders*, who was sacked because of the employer's worry that potential customers would feel uneasy if he were near their children. Note that it is certainly unlawful for your employer to sack you because customers or other workers object to your race or gender.

- Criminal activity occurs outside work which makes the employee unsuitable. It is important to note that your employer has an obligation to consider carefully whether the offence really makes you unsuitable for your employment.

Perhaps the most interesting and surprising circumstance is that you may fairly be dismissed for a criminal offence committed outside your employment. The fairness of the **dismissal** does not depend upon whether you have been imprisoned for the crime and are therefore unable to attend work, but upon whether the commission of the offence makes you an unsuitable employee. Imagine that you worked in a pharmacy, or as a youth worker, and you committed even a minor drugs or sexual offence, or as a check-out operator and you committed an offence of dishonesty involving cash.

- Business reorganisation.

## An appropriate sanction?

Consider the following case – the facts follow a real case quite closely.

### Bert and the hyacinth bulbs

Bert was a supervisor working for a transport company. He had worked for the company for 20 years. Part of his job was to ensure that there were no thefts from the site. One day the company was transporting a number of net bags of hyacinth bulbs. One of these bags fell off a pallet and split open.

Bert inspected the damage and decided, quite reasonably, that the bag was a total loss. Imagine – bulbs all over the floor, some broken, some crushed, some missing and the bag damaged beyond repair. Bert filled in the form for a loss and asked one of the workers to clear up the mess and throw the bulbs away

At the end of the shift, Bert looked into the bin and decided that half a dozen of the bulbs were not too badly damaged, so he pocketed them. His manager saw him and, following a hearing, dismissed him.

In the real case – which is not reported in the law reports – it does not set a **precedent**; the tribunal found in Bert's favour. It agreed with the employer that the reason Bert was dismissed was **potentially fair** on the grounds of his (mis)conduct – he had taken something belonging to the firm – but held that the firm had not taken sufficient notice of his good conduct and long service. The tribunal held that the firm had acted very harshly and had itself breached the standard of behaviour laid down in precedent for employers to follow. The leading case in this matter is *Iceland Frozen Foods v Jones*, and it lays down guidance for **employment tribunals** to follow in assessing whether employers have appropriately applied the ultimate sanction of **dismissal**. The *Iceland* test requires the tribunal to consider how a reasonable employer would behave faced with the facts before it. The tribunal must not consider how its own members would behave in that situation, but must ask whether the employer's response fell within the *range of reasonable responses* of an employer. If the employer's response in dismissing the employee falls within that range, it does not matter whether the tribunal finds it harsh, unfair or unfeeling: the dismissal is fair.

Recently, the *Iceland* test has come under attack in the tribunal, and for a short time it was replaced by a test which required the tribunal to be more active and consider whether, in the light of the members' experience of working life, the employer had acted fairly in dismissing the employee. This test, derived from *Haddon v Van den Bergh Foods Ltd*, looked as if it would revolutionise the practice of **employment tribunals**. However, the Court of Appeal returned to the fray and in a pair of cases, *Post Office v Foley* and *HSBC Bank plc v Madden*, upheld the *Iceland* test. The ball is still in play because one applicant who was caught in the middle of the time period between the *Haddon* and *Foley/Madden* cases has entered an application to the European Court of Human Rights to have the matter looked at again. We mention this because this latest case will, if it is successful, shake **employment tribunal** practice to its roots, but also, in the meantime, it allows us to explain the real key to understanding the *Iceland* test.

## Mr B the printer

Some facts are necessary. Mr B worked for a printing firm. Mr B said that a fellow employee attacked him whilst he was working; the employer said that Mr B and another employee were fighting at work. The employer said, fairly enough, that fighting in a print shop is extremely dangerous and, following an investigation, dismissed both employees. Now the facts become a little confused, because on one reading of the employer's decision it appears that they thought that Mr B was the victim rather than the aggressor. Nevertheless, the employer dismissed Mr B. The tribunal found that the employer's decision was harsh, but as an employer could reasonably come to the decision to dismiss on the facts as the printing firm had found them, then the **dismissal** must be fair. Mr B now said, 'Hang about, Article 6 of the European Convention on Human Rights gives me the right to have my case heard by an *independent* tribunal. If the tribunal is bound by the *Iceland* case to judge me by the standards of a *reasonable employer*, it is *not* an *independent* tribunal ...'. We are still awaiting a decision as to whether the European Court of Human Rights is going to give Mr B's case a full hearing because there are a lot of complex legal arguments lurking in the undergrowth of this difficult case. However, we hope that our simplification makes the point of *Iceland* clear: if the employer behaved as a reasonable employer then the dismissal is fair.

## Was the decision to dismiss arrived at in a fair way?

We must again look at some **precedents**. The two most important cases are *British Home Stores* and *Polkey v AE Dayton Services*. There is also some very new **statutory** material. Let's look at the gist of the *Polkey* case – its facts are fairly shocking. One Friday afternoon Denis Polkey arrived back at his employer's premises. He had been out doing his job delivering parts in the firm's van. When he arrived back at the depot, the boss said, 'Take your mate home, he's just been made redundant'. So Polkey did so, no doubt railing with his mate about the iniquities of employers. He returned to the office and the boss said, '... and you are redundant too' – no consultation, no discussion, no warning, just *go home* (that's a crossword clue – the answer has seven letters, two words, beginning and ending with 'f').

Before you ask us to wash our mouths out with soap, please consider: that's really what is being said here isn't it? Mr Polkey is not being treated with dignity, respect, kindness or courtesy is he? The employer might as well have told him to f*** **f.

The problem for Mr Polkey was that the employer really did need to make the employees **redundant** to save the business. The substantive decision to dismiss seems to fall within the rule in *Iceland*. However, the courts (in fact, the highest court of all, the House of Lords) came to Mr Polkey's rescue and gave him some compensation. They said that not only must a **dismissal** be substantively fair, it must be *procedurally* fair. What does having a fair procedure mean? Here the law has recently been changed, having been amended by the Employment Act 2002. 'Acting fairly' means, in essence, that the employer:

- must tell you clearly about the threat to your continued employment so that you realise the severity of the situation and can get your case in order;

- has a duty to investigate the circumstances of the case – the employer has to find proper objective and demonstrable grounds on which to base a decision to dismiss;

- must, having given proper warning and reasonable notice, hold a disciplinary hearing at which you can put forward your explanation, with the help of a representative if you want one;

Always take a representative with you to any disciplinary hearing. This is usually a colleague or trade union representative. You are rarely permitted to bring someone from outside the workplace and, in 30 years' experience on 'both sides of the fence', Bob has only seen a solicitor allowed in on three occasions. A friend or colleague helps you to keep your cool in a stressful situation, they can take notes and they may remember some important fact you missed.

o give you the opportunity to have a fair disciplinary hearing – this normally means that someone not directly connected with the case will hear it (for example, a manager from another department) and the rules of natural justice will be applied (that is, you will be given a copy of the procedure to be followed, etc);

o must, in the hearing, allow you to question the employer's witnesses and must allow you to bring witnesses in support of your own side of the story;

o must consider whether dismissal was an appropriate sanction or whether, for example, redeployment was an acceptable option.

If you are dismissed, your employer should give you the opportunity to appeal – and the appeals officer should be someone fresh to the case.

Large, well organised employers will often have a **contractual** disciplinary procedure which has been negotiated with a trade union and this may well contain a number of other safeguards. If you are employed by a small employer it is possible, or likely, that the disciplinary procedure is rather simple. However, the recent amendments to the Employment Rights Act 1996 provide that if your employer does not have any sort of disciplinary procedure, or if its provisions fail to reach a statutory minimum, then any dismissal will be **automatically unfair**.

One might say that what one gains on the swings one loses on the roundabouts, because the same set of amendments also provide that, where the disciplinary procedure is of at least the statutory standard, any minor breach of the disciplinary procedure will not render the dismissal unfair.

To remind you, the leading cases are *Polkey v AE Dayton Services* (1987) IRLR 503 and *Iceland Frozen Foods v Jones* (1982) IRLR 43. However, the law of **unfair dismissal**, which restricts the right of employers to dismiss **qualified employees** for no good reason, was first introduced in 1971. A huge number of legal **precedents** have grown up over the years and some of the legal doctrines are still matters of controversy in the courts. Do consider carefully whether you ought to get professional legal help in the **employment tribunal**, especially if you know that the other side will be represented by a solicitor or barrister.

# 17

# Redundancy

In the previous chapter we mentioned redundancy; it is now time to deal with this more fully. Redundancy is a special case in the law governing **unfair dismissal**, because it is a **potentially fair reason for dismissal**.

The **statutory** definition of redundancy is in s 139 of the Employment Rights Act (ERA) 1996, and we repeat it here from Chapter 16:

For an employee to be **redundant**:

o     the employer must have ceased, or intend to cease, to carry on the business completely, or in the place where the employee was employed; or

o     the business must have discontinued or reduced the amount of the work which the employee was employed to do.

In other words, redundancy means that you are dismissed because your employer does not need the 'job' any more.

This is what makes redundancy 'special' – nobody is getting at you personally. The other reasons for fair dismissal – typically 'capacity' (or lack of capacity) and 'conduct' (or misconduct) – apply personally to *you*, your health or your wrongdoing. 'Redundancy' applies to *the job*, whoever has been doing it. Since redundancy is one of the potentially fair reasons for dismissal, it is subject to the normal rules of fairness set out in Chapter 16, but modified to take account of the differences between redundancy and the 'personal' reasons for **dismissal**. Thus if:

o     your employer has correctly identified the situation as being one of redundancy; *and*

o     your employer has used a fair means for selecting you for redundancy; *and* o    your employer has used a fair procedure in implementing your redundancy,

you may lawfully be dismissed.

However, quite unlike other forms of fair dismissal, if your employer dismisses you for the reason of redundancy you are entitled to compensation, provided that your redundancy passes the following tests.

## Has your employer correctly identified the situation as being one of redundancy?

Look at s 139 of the ERA 1996. Has your job ceased to exist? Your employer may well have decided to abolish it in order to save money and that is quite within his rights – provided that it is a genuine **redundancy**. Strictly speaking, it is *not* a redundancy if the employer sacks one person and then gets their colleague to work twice as hard.

The problem with challenging this situation for the individual worker is that the employer has greater power and more information. The employer can generally find a way to convince a tribunal that this is a genuine redundancy. Furthermore, there is always the question of solidarity: will the person who is kept on really undertake to do twice as much work? Some people say this situation is exactly what trade unions are for – and indeed this might well account for the special position of trade unions in redundancy law. If you think that this is going on, the trade union is the only organisation that can help you – but unions don't work too well for just one person in a workplace.

## Has your employer used a fair means for selecting you for redundancy?

The old way of selecting people for redundancy was known as LIFO: last in – first out. If you had only held the job for a short time, you were the first person to be sacked. This technique was extensively used during the era of collective *laissez-faire* (see Chapter 1, p 9), but disappeared during the era of individual rights (p 10).

During the mass-production era you had lots of people doing identical jobs, turning out widgets on production lines. A downturn in the market for widgets meant a drop in the demand for widget makers; and LIFO ruled OK. Times have changed. LIFO no longer applies and now employers are able to use whatever rational means they choose to select jobs for redundancy.

Let us illustrate: Bob used to work in a major university as a senior biochemistry technician. He was also the senior union officer. The university employed people to look at high speed cine-camera films of cloud chamber traces used in atom-smashing experiments. These people were called scanners. New technology was introduced and the scanners were made **redundant**, even though the university was taking on staff in other areas. (Eventually Bob was made redundant himself – because the department in which he worked didn't need so many technicians – so Bob went off and retrained as a legal academic.)

The widget makers and the scanners had one point in common: their employers had clear criteria for making people redundant – they needed people with certain skills to run their business, and when their needs changed they were left with a surplus of workers whose skills were no longer useful to them. It was impossible to challenge the employer because the employer demonstrated the use of rational criteria in selection.

## Has your employer used a fair procedure in putting your redundancy into force?

The essence of a fair procedure in any fair **dismissal** is some form of consultation. As we have seen, if you are likely to be dismissed for some sort of *personal* reason – misconduct or incapacity – the employer has to talk to you about it.

If the employer wants to dismiss you because you are **redundant**, he has to talk about it not only to you, but also to your trade union representative (or whoever has been elected to deal with redundancy consultation).

Here, however, we are only dealing with individual rights so we will stick to individual consultation. The main point that your employer has to consult you about is whether you can be redeployed to do a different job, with or without some retraining.

The university scanners were mostly redeployed into different jobs – some of them (rather ironically) into building the new technology which was designed to replace them. Others were deployed into some very different jobs indeed – for example, one of them was helped to return to nursing with an associated employer. There may be all sorts of ways that an individual can avoid redundancy – job sharing, flexible working, reorganising the job completely; as well as the most obvious way of being slotted into a vacancy that may arise. Bob did not want to be redeployed, so he took his compensation money and rode off into the sunset.

If you are fairly made redundant, two types of compensation may be available to you.

## Statutory compensation

This is compensation set by law. How do you calculate this? You can find the answer on the Department of Trade and Industry (DTI) website under www.dti.gov.uk/er/redundancy, where they provide a useful ready-reckoner. At the time of writing, the maximum amount of *statutory* compensation is £7,800, which is calculated on the basis of one week's pay (capped at £260) per year of employment for people aged 40 and under, and one-and-a-half week's pay for people aged 41 and over (capped at £390). There is an overall cap of £7,800. This site also contains lots of further reading about redundancy.

## Company redundancy schemes

Your employer may have offered a **contractual redundancy** scheme or may have negotiated one with the trade union. If you join such a scheme, you are entitled to its benefits. Typical contractual redundancy schemes offer one full week's pay, rather than £260 per week, as the basis of calculation; or it may offer, say, two weeks' pay per actual year of service. In 1985, Bob was offered, and accepted, one month's actual (cf one week's capped) pay per year of service together with a bonus payment. This was very helpful in funding his legal studies. It is quite common for employers to ask you to agree that any payment made under a more generous company scheme will be taken to *include* your **statutory** entitlement. This stops you having two bites at the cherry.

The good news is that payments of up to £30,000 are free from tax and National Insurance contributions under s 148 of the Income and Corporation Taxes Act 1988.

You are also entitled to other non-cash benefits, such as time off to look for another job. There are also special requirements for consultation with trade unions or other employees' representatives.

Unfortunately, some employers use the special feature of 'redundancy' – the fact that it carries an automatic right to compensation – to act as a shield or cover for other forms of **dismissal**, reasoning that if an employee gets a little bit of compensation, they are likely to 'go quietly'.

Fortunately, this group of employers is very much in the minority and they should not be allowed to use redundancy to cheat employees out of compensation. If you are the victim of a sham redundancy – you are dismissed and the employer immediately employs someone else to do your old job – you may go to the **employment tribunal** and make a claim for **unfair dismissal**, in which case you may be entitled to additional compensation.

---

No one doubts that, from time to time, it is best for employers and employees to decide to terminate their relationship, but there are special legal mechanisms for doing so and they are there to be used.

---

# Constructive dismissal and wrongful dismissal

We have discussed **constructive dismissal** and **wrongful dismissal** together because they share important legal features. Whilst constructive dismissal is a **statutory** claim and wrongful dismissal is a common law (or **precedent**-based) claim, both claims depend upon the employer breaching the **contract of employment**.

Constructive dismissal is said to occur when your employer makes life at work so difficult for you that you can legitimately say that he has shown by his conduct that the contract between employer and employee is at an end. This has to be a serious breach – in 'law-speak', it must be fundamental; it must go to the root of the contract. This has an important implication. You may then walk out and claim that you have been unfairly and constructively dismissed.

---

The test applied by the courts and tribunals is extremely strict. Do not just walk out and expect to win massive compensation. Read the examples given below and assess your chances. You may wish to take professional legal advice.

---

## 'Big Tits'

In *Insitu Cleaning Services v Heads*, Ms Heads came into work where she was met by the boss's son with the unusual greeting, 'Hiya Big Tits'. We know ladies (our Rosy included) who would have been amused and/or flattered, or responded with 'Hi, Wee Willie', but Ms Head was deeply offended and complained.

We are not having a cheap crack at Ms Heads, we are making an important legal point. Harassment cases turn on the point of whether the person affected was reasonable in finding the words or action offensive, unwanted and unwarranted.

Clearly some people do find this expression offensive, whilst others would not be offended even by a much cruder turn of phrase. The question seems to be: would a reasonable person be offended? (A court has held that reasonable people would not be offended by 'pin-up' pictures of naked women which do not show the pubic region. *Stewart v Cleveland Guest Engineering* is the precedent for this proposition.)

The employer agreed that it was a serious matter and asked her to make a formal complaint, whereupon they would investigate and, if her case was proved, they would take action. Ms Heads decided *not* to make a formal complaint and resigned instead, claiming that she had been the victim of sex **discrimination** and that she had been **constructively dismissed**.

The tribunal agreed that she had been the victim of sex discrimination and awarded her compensation for her hurt feelings, but held that she had not been constructively dismissed because the employer had offered her a way to restore the working relationship. The employer had shown, said the tribunal, that they would respect Ms Head's **contractual** rights by giving her a proper forum in which to complain; and they had made it clear that they would take action against the offender.

This case should be compared with *Bracebridge Engineering v Darby*, in which a single serious indecent assault was sufficient to allow the complainant to succeed in her action for **constructive dismissal**. This is the hand-up-the-employee's-skirt case we discussed in Chapter 4 (p 34).

The test applied by the tribunals seems to be three-fold:

○ Was there a breach of the **contract of employment** by the employer? If so, then the employee has an arguable case; if not, then the employee's claim fails.

o   Can the employer do anything to make amends? If they cannot put things right (*Bracebridge Engineering*), the complainant must win; if they can put things right, move to the next question.

o   Has the employer taken reasonable steps to resolve the situation? If so, the complainant must lose (*Insitu Cleaning Services*).

The modern cases on constructive dismissal turn, in the main, upon proving allegations that the employer had breached the **implied term** of the contract of employment that 'mutual trust and confidence' should be maintained (see Chapter 4). Cases in this area range from the demotion of a worker, through a worker being treated badly and insulted in front of a subordinate, on to the infliction of irreparable damage to a worker's professional reputation.

The point that the employer's breach has to be fundamental in order to create a constructive dismissal also means that the employee who feels that this is the case has very little time in which to act. Suppose that you wish to allege that your employer fundamentally breached your contract 12 months ago – if so, was it really fundamental? You took a long time working that out, didn't you? Even if it was, as a matter of law, a fundamental breach, it is likely that the tribunal would say that you condoned the breach – you did not treat it as a fundamental breach. The point about a breach which 'goes to the root of the contract' is that you must treat it as such and *walk out as soon as possible*. OK, the tribunals are realistic and will give you a short period of grace in which to get another job – but if you take more than just a few days you had better have a very good reason; otherwise the tribunal is likely to hold that you simply resigned.

# Wrongful dismissal

At common law, rather than under the **statutory** provisions set out in the Employment Rights Act 1996, either party to a **contract of employment** can end the contract without giving a reason simply by giving **contractual** notice, that is, the period of notice set out in the contract of employment.

The common law provisions rule the contract until the statutory right not to be **unfairly dismissed** cuts in after one year of **continuous employment**; furthermore, the common law continues to apply throughout the contract.

This means that if your employer dismisses you without giving you contractual notice, unless you have indicated by your conduct that you no longer intend to be bound by the contract, you can sue for the pay you would have received during the period of notice.

Here are three examples which illustrate the law on unfair dismissal.

## Lager lout?

John has been employed by Nadir Ltd for eight months as a van driver. One lunchtime at work, in contravention both of the law and of the terms of his **contract of employment**, he goes to the pub and drinks five pints of Export lager. He drives away from the pub in an erratic manner and is stopped by the police and breathalysed. He is arrested and charged with 'drink-driving'. His employer dismisses him immediately.

This is known as a **summary dismissal** and it is without notice or pay in lieu of notice. This is lawful. John may not successfully claim for **wrongful dismissal**.

## Sticky fingers?

Mary has been employed by Abyss Ltd for six months as a shop assistant. One day the employer finds that a member of staff has been stealing from the till. The employer responds by sacking all the assistants summarily. Mary may recover her pay in lieu of her **contractual** notice and may recover other sums in respect of her losses – for example, contractual overtime and bonus and any pay deducted allegedly in respect of losses.

## Martyred manager?

Hilary has been employed as the manager of Womanchester Thursday Football Club for three years. WTFC are firmly fixed at the bottom of Division 2 of the league and are facing relegation. The directors decide to sack Hilary, whose **contract of employment** carries an entitlement to two years' notice. They want Hilary to go now. If they don't pay her two years' salary in lieu of notice, Hilary will succeed in a claim for **wrongful dismissal**.

Hilary has the option of taking the matter to the county court (or the High Court in London for very large sums) or the **employment tribunal**. Since football managers earn megabucks, she had best check the current limit on contract claims in the employment tribunal. Call **ACAS** (details in 'Buzzwords', p xv) to find out, Hilary!

# Compensation for dismissal or redundancy

In this chapter, we consider compensation for **dismissal**. Other forms of compensation which might be payable (such as for **discrimination**) are discussed later.

## Wrongful dismissal

If you are **wrongfully dismissed**, you are entitled to the pay and other benefits you would have received under your contract during your notice period. You do not get non-contractual or discretionary benefits. In other words, you have the right to what your contract says you are entitled to, and nothing more. This may seem mean, but that is the way the law works. The problem with wrongful dismissal is that the claim is based in common law (**precedent**), not **statute** law; and under common law an employer has the right to bring a **contract of employment** to an end simply by giving notice.

## Unfair dismissal

If you are **unfairly dismissed**, the tribunal will assess compensation. They will make a *basic* award equal to the amount of **statutory** redundancy pay you would have received if you had fairly been made **redundant**, and will then make a *compensatory* award which is an 'intelligent guess' (based on a lot of experience and knowledge!) as to the amount you would have been paid if you had not been unfairly dismissed. To put it crudely, this means:

○ How many months will you be out of work until you get another job which pays the same salary?

○ What other benefits have you lost?

○ What about your pension? (There are regulations to help with the calculation of the pension component.)

You can find details of the limits on the amounts that can be awarded by clicking onto the Department of Trade and Industry (DTI) website at www.dti.gov.uk/er and following the links. Notice that in certain cases there are minimum awards (such as for expulsion from a trade union) and there is an overall cap on payments. At the time of writing, the total payment (basic and compensatory award) was something over £60,000, *but* do not think that if you get the sack from your paper round you are going to be awarded £60,000! The amount you get is tied closely to your pay and to the likelihood of your getting another job: so, for example, a 54-year-old general manager would get more compensation than a 24-year-old secretary.

However, there is another kind of limit on your compensation for **unfair dismissal** – you are subject to a duty to *mitigate* your loss. You cannot just get the sack, then sit around waiting for your compensation cheque to arrive. You have to try to get another job.

This does *not* mean that you have to take just any old job – you have to apply for jobs within a reasonable travelling distance, which are appropriate to your qualifications and experience, and which pay a reasonable salary.

---

Apply for jobs – and keep copies of the advertisements and your applications – because your employer and their representative can ask the tribunal to look at these at any hearing.

---

# Redundancy

Redundancy is a little more complex. OK, you are entitled to a maximum of £7,800 in compensation, but the 'duty to mitigate' arises even *before* you are dismissed.

Thus, if you are **redundant**, you are entitled to a redundancy payment, except in the following circumstances (all references are to the Employment Rights Act 1996).

(Section 140) You are dismissed for misconduct during the period of redundancy notice.

(Section 141) You refuse a reasonable offer to renew your **contract of employment** or to **re-engage** you on a new contract.

Your employer can make this offer *either:*

o   as soon as your current contract comes to an end; *or*

o   not more than four weeks after the end of your current contract.

After that, if:

o   the employment on offer is suitable; *and*

o   you unreasonably refuse it,

you lose your right to a redundancy payment.

The law sets the rules for assessing what is and what is not a reasonable offer of suitable employment, and the courts have thoroughly explored these rules. Broadly speaking, if the job you are offered has similar terms and conditions, critically including:

o   pay;

o   hours; and

o   place of work,

it is a reasonable offer.

---

You have four weeks to try out the new job; if you find that it is unsuitable, you still have the right to a redundancy payment.

---

(Section 142) You give your employer notice that you wish to leave early (for example, to start a new job), and your employer gives you a **statutory** request, requiring you to work out the notice period, and you refuse to do so.

The withholding of the redundancy payment in this case may be challenged at the **employment tribunal**, which may order your employer to pay part of it.

(Section 143) You go on strike during a period of statutory redundancy notice, and your employer extends your notice period to make up for the days when you are on strike – and you refuse to work those days.

The withholding of the redundancy payment in this case may be challenged at the employment tribunal, which may order your employer to pay part of it.

If your employer does not give you your **redundancy** money because he has become insolvent ('gone bust'), you are entitled to take the claim not against your employer but against the Secretary of State. The procedure is given in s 166 of the Employment Rights Act 1996.

Incidentally, similar provisions apply under Part XII of the Employment Rights Act 1996 with regard to debts of:

o   wages;

o   pay during notice period;

o   holiday pay; and/or

o   **unfair dismissal** compensation,

which remain unpaid because of the insolvency of your employer.

# PART 4

# THE EMPLOYMENT TRIBUNAL AND THE LAW

# 20

# The last resort – the employment tribunal

Let's assume you have a grievance. You have done your homework. You have pushed all the right buttons. Your grievance is still unresolved and you have decided to take your employer to an **employment tribunal**. Sighing deeply, you reach for form IT1.

IT in this context is short for 'industrial tribunal'. The tribunal changed its name to '**employment tribunal**' several years ago, but the form number stayed the same.

You can find a sample form IT1 at the back of this book. Before you fill it in, however, you should read the literature on the subject. This is available:

o    from your local Job Centre or Citizens Advice Bureau (CAB);

o    on the internet at www.employmenttribunals.gov.uk;

o    from the Employment Tribunals Service enquiry line, telephone number 0845 795 9775.

One leaflet, *What To Do if Taken to an Employment Tribunal*, is particularly aimed towards employers, but it is still worth reading because you need to know what the employer is expected to do to answer your claim.

Other leaflets cover *How to Apply to an Employment Tribunal, Hearings at Employment Tribunals, Having Your Say* and *Putting Things Right*. They explain your right to expenses for yourself and any witnesses you call, as well as giving guidance on the employment tribunal itself.

These are good, clear leaflets. *How to Apply to an Employment Tribunal* even has a page of 'buzzwords'. For example, you will be the 'Applicant', your employer will be the 'Respondent' and you will be attending a 'Hearing'.

## How to apply to an employment tribunal

Here we set out the bare minimum of advice. Before starting down this track, *do consider whether the time has come to get professional advice.*

Complete the application form IT1. You can do this online on the employment tribunals website at www.employmenttribunals.gov.uk or post a paper form to the nearest **employment tribunals** office. You will find a list on pp 17–18 of *How to Apply to an Employment Tribunal,* which is available either as a paper booklet from your local Job Centre or CAB or on the employment tribunals website (see above). Make sure you keep a copy for your own records.

You can also e-mail your form – see p 20 of *How to Apply to an Employment Tribunal* for the e-mail addresses of the various offices.

1    If form-filling is not your forte (Rosy hyperventilates at the sight of the simplest form), ask your trade union representative to help, or call in at your local CAB. Alternatively, if you are going to get a solicitor to act for you, ask the solicitor to fill in the form, because if there are differences between what you write in the IT1 and what you write or say later or at the tribunal, the Respondent will pick up on it and exploit the differences.

2    Getting the application in on time (the deadline is almost invariably *three months from the date your employment ended*) is your responsibility. There are also time limits for claims for **redundancy** payments. Call the Redundancy Payment Helpline, telephone number 0500 848 489, for guidance.

Mark in your diary a date at least a week ahead of the three-month deadline to make sure you don't miss the boat. This is *vital* (see below).

*Do not think that this three-month deadline is only a guideline – it is fixed and rigorously enforced.* One applicant posted an application through the door of the **employment tribunal** after the office had closed on the last day for applications (a Friday), thus the application was not stamped as received until the following Monday. It was ruled *out of time*. So if you are late, the Respondent will apply for it to be ruled out *and will almost certainly succeed.*

## Where will your tribunal be held?

There are numerous venues, and where your hearing will be held depends on your postcode. The guide on pp 17–18 of *How to Apply to an Employment Tribunal* allocates a centre to every postcode. (Both Rosy and Bob would have to go to Bury St Edmunds. Like everyone else, they would receive a letter from the Service with a map showing the location of the hearing and details of local parking and refreshment facilities. The latter are fairly basic, so take a packed lunch and a flask!)

## What happens when you apply?

The first thing that is likely to happen is that you will receive a simple acknowledgment from the **employment tribunal**. If your application is wildly late, or contains obvious and gross errors, you may get a letter saying that a Chairman of the Tribunal has considered it and is calling upon you to attend a hearing.

This is serious. You *must* go and you should consider getting a professional representative to go with you. If you just ignore the letter, you will not be allowed to continue with your claim.

However, a letter from the Chairman is pretty unlikely. It is far more likely that your application will clear the first hurdle and that you will be told that the application has been forwarded to the Respondent, who has 21 days in which to reply.

This 21-day period can be extended if the Respondent asks for extra time. When your former employer responds, you will be sent a copy of their formal response (called an IT3). This will not make a pleasant 'read' – sit down, take a deep breath and a glass of cold water, then read it.

If the Respondent has taken professional advice, you will be called (in icily polite euphemisms) a liar and a cheat and it will be alleged that, when you deigned to work at all, you were almost totally useless. If the Respondent has done a DIY job, you will get the same – but it will not be so polite!

Do not worry about this. What did you really expect your former employer to say? Since either:

o    they dismissed you in the first place; or

o    they treated you so badly that you felt the contract was at an end,

it is plain that they are not going to welcome you back with flowers and chocolates and say nice things about you. However, if things go well and the Respondent says that it was all an awful mistake, you might like to consider talking to **ACAS** (the Advisory, Conciliation and Arbitration Service) about getting yourself **reinstated**.

About a week later, you will receive a letter from the tribunal (unless it was enclosed with the IT3), giving 'Directions'. You must read this letter, and the leaflet which comes with it, very carefully.

'Directions' is the list of things you *must* do in preparation for the hearing, rather than how to find the venue. The tribunal requires you to get your papers in order, and to correspond with the Respondent, in order to produce a *bundle* for the *hearing*. A bundle is law-speak for all the documents that you propose to rely on. The tribunal will ask you and the Respondent to agree a joint bundle (all papers indexed in chronological order) for the hearing, and to sort out how you are going to produce six copies. Do *not* be awkward about this. Try to co-operate and get it done.

Some people play all sorts of disreputable tricks at this stage – 'paper-bombing', 'interlocutory orders' and all sorts of nonsense. Do not get involved in this unless you are very experienced; it is just tedious.

The tribunal will have set a date for a hearing. This is to be considered fixed unless you have a very good reason. If you genuinely can't make that date, *tell the tribunal at once* and apply for a postponement.

The next thing to happen is that you will get a call from ACAS. About 90% of **employment tribunal** claims are settled by ACAS officers. An ACAS officer will ring you and set up an appointment to meet. ACAS officers are neutral – they do not work for the employer, they do not work for the tribunal, neither do they work for you. Their job is to try to resolve the matter without it going to a hearing, either by setting up a conciliation meeting between you and the Respondent or by seeing if you can both agree on a **termination**/compensation package.

ACAS officers are almost invariably wonderful and are widely recognised for their mediation skills and professional approach. Bob remembers going in front of one tribunal in the East End of London on a difficult case. When he and the solicitor acting for the Respondent said that, following a chat in the waiting room, they were going back to ACAS, they almost received a round of applause.

The ACAS officer assigned to your case will explain what they are able to do, and will ask whether you would like them to try to reach a settlement between you and the Respondent.

There is one very important point which you must remember. ACAS is totally independent of the tribunal, and their discussions are completely private; indeed you are not allowed to say things like 'The ACAS officer said …' to the tribunal. If you agree to let ACAS try to help you and the Respondent to settle matters, it will not prejudice your (or the Respondent's) case in any way – unless you opt for 'binding conciliation', in which case the ACAS solution will be binding on both you and your former employer and you will be blocked from taking action in the tribunal. Do consider whether ACAS might be able to find an advantageous way out of the problem.

## The hearing

You will find that your hearing is timetabled for '10 am or as soon as possible thereafter' on a given day. Turn up at no later than 9.30 am, and earlier if you can possibly make it – it is quite likely that the employer or their representative will wish to speak to you. Go to the Applicants' Waiting Room or to the Reception Desk – you may need to fill in some forms concerning attendance. Anyhow, somewhere you will be booked in by a clerk.

We wouldn't dream of telling you what to wear, but the tribunal is, after all, a court of law, and understated, business-like clothes would be appropriate.

You will be called into the Tribunal Room. At a raised table you will find three people dressed in business clothes – no wigs or gowns. The one in the centre is the Chair. He or she is addressed as Sir or Madam and is in charge of the proceedings. The Chair is an experienced barrister or solicitor. The two Wing Members who flank the Chair are representatives of industry – typically a local trade unionist and a local member of the Chamber of Commerce.

For **discrimination** cases you will always find, as appropriate, representatives of an ethnic minority race, or both sexes, or someone living with a disability. You will be asked to sit and the Chair will explain the outline of the procedure. If you are unrepresented, you are known as an *Applicant in person* and the Chair will give you some procedural help – but no favours.

This is a 'legal hearing' and the tribunal is completely unbiased. You will be sworn according to your faith, or you may affirm that you will tell the truth. Of course you *must* tell the truth in court, unless you want to end up like Jeffrey Archer!

You are the Applicant, so you go first. It is best to have a written witness statement, which will begin 'I am [Bob Watt] and this is my evidence', and to read it to the tribunal. As far as you can, keep your eyes on the tribunal – they are assessing your credibility.

When you have finished, the Respondent will be invited to ask you questions and the tribunal may well have some questions of their own. Answer the other side's questions as briefly and precisely as possible, because they are trying to trap you into making damaging admissions. Be a little more forthcoming with the tribunal, because they can and will keep going until they have a clear picture of the case. You may then call your witnesses, if any.

The scene then shifts to the other side. They give their evidence and you are given the opportunity to question it. Do remember that this is a court of law and that expressions like 'You ******* liar' will damage your case! 'That is not how I remember it' is far more helpful.

After all the evidence has been given, you and the Respondent will get the opportunity to put submissions – points of law.

Then the tribunal gives you its decision.

This is only a very brief summary, and we hope that it sounds rather daunting! The point is that all the evidence obtained by researchers shows that applicants who are represented at a tribunal have a far higher chance of success. This is not because the issues of law are particularly difficult, but because the people who do this sort of work all day every day have much more knowledge and skill in picking out the important issues and presenting the salient facts to the tribunal.

---

The tribunal is fundamentally a tribunal of fact and will be interested in what happened and when. Getting everything in order takes some experience. Furthermore, someone who is not emotionally involved (in the way that you are sure to be) is much more likely to present the case clearly and convincingly. So, unless you are used to making quite charged presentations in front of a potentially hostile audience, you would do well to consider getting professional representation.

---

# Some thoughts about the law

In general, this book is practical rather than contemplative. Here, however, we pause for thought and our first thought is this: what is the point of writing a book about the law for lay people? There are plenty of trained lawyers about and, if one is dealing with valuable things, like one's rights – especially the right to a job, which is probably the most valuable thing you ever have – doesn't it make sense to go to an expert? Even if you earn only £20,000 per year, that adds up to £1 million over a working lifetime. Not even the most hardened do-it-yourself fanatic would try to mend a £1 million machine that had broken down.

Now Rosy likes to speak in parables, and when Bob showed her this paragraph she said: 'OK, that's fine; but if you own an expensive piece of kit, you need to know roughly how it works and how to make simple adjustments. You will then operate it more sensitively and you will know which problems you can deal with yourself and which need the professionals with their knowledge and their experience and their sophisticated test gear. Take my big old Hewlett Packard laser printer. If I couldn't do a spot of rudimentary trouble-shooting I'd be forever calling in the repair man. As it is, I've had nearly 10 years' service out of it. And, unless you have this rudimentary, layman's knowledge, your lawyer, plumber or car mechanic could get everything disastrously wrong, at terrifying expense to you, and you'd be none the wiser. That's the whole point of this series. We show you how to identify the problems you can sort out for yourself, and we tell you when to consider calling in the experts.'

Be that as it may, we decided to write a few paragraphs about the philosophy of law to try to explain what we have been doing. Indeed, one prominent legal philosopher, John Harris, says that the whole point of lawyers studying the philosophy of law is to enable them to give a justification for what they do.

Let's start with some undeniable facts about the law.

The law tells us what we *ought* to do. When we say *ought*, we don't mean it in the sense that we *ought* to love our neighbour because that is how we become good, even though a lot of people use *ought* in that way and some philosophers of law insist that it is the only meaningful way in which we can say *ought*.

Our understanding of *ought* is more pragmatic and self-interested. We use *ought* in the sense that we ought to do something because that way we avoid the pitfalls and penalties – losing our job, having to pay compensation, being put in prison, and so on. We could even make that statement more sophisticated and say that the law advises us on what we *ought to do if we want to keep out of trouble*.

We might get away with breaking the law, and we might even think that the penalty for breaking the law is less than the cost of continuing to observe the law. From a purely practical point of view, this attitude makes sense in employment law. Sometimes employers think that it is cheaper to sack an employee and pay compensation for breaking the rules, than to keep the employee on.

So (and thus far we have followed the outline of the reasoning of two famous philosophers of law, Hans Kelsen and Joseph Raz), if the law tells us what we ought to do (and how others ought to behave towards us), then it must have some distinguishing characteristics. It is these characteristics that make it the law.

How do we know what these characteristics are? What is the law trying to do? It is trying to guide our behaviour, of course. If the law is trying to guide our behaviour, we need to understand what it is saying to us. Secret laws are no use – nobody can blame you for lighting up in a public place unless there is a NO SMOKING sign somewhere; nor are retrospective laws – laws passed today which tell us what we ought to have done yesterday. Fortunately, both of those categories of law are very rare indeed.

However, the third formal description of law often poses a problem for ordinary people. To be any use at all, the law has to be clear. If citizens do not act in accordance with the law simply because they cannot understand the way it is set out, it is not law (or at the very least, and following Hans Kelsen, it's a 'pathology of law'). In this book we are trying to make one small area of the law clear, to enable you to avoid the pitfalls and the penalties.

The law can be unclear in two ways. First, it can be unclear in the sense that whoever wrote it made such a bad job of drafting the law that the reader is trapped in an impenetrable tangle of prose. That is unforgivable. What do we pay politicians and civil servants for? However, it still happens from time to time. An example is in the area of maternity leave. Simon Deakin and Gillian Morris, two leading commentators on employment law, state in *Labour Law* (Butterworths, 1998) that: 'In 1981 Browne-Wilkinson J described the provisions relating to maternity leave (which were considerably less convoluted than those now in force) as being of "inordinate complexity exceeding the worst excesses of a taxing statute", a criticism endorsed by the Court of Appeal'.

Wow! This seems to suggest that there are times when you should not try to understand the inner workings of the law, but rather let those whose business it is (trade unions, maternity rights organisations and so forth) wrestle with them. If you are pregnant, you can use our book, and the www.tiger.gov.uk (the tailored interactive guidance on employment rights website) calculator, to find out what you are personally entitled to, and let the professionals argue about the details. You have a baby on the way and you have far more important things to do than bother about the complexities of the law! We will return to this point in a short while.

A sub-class of this kind of lack of clarity occurs where judges fail adequately to explain the law. Rare – but it does happen. By far the worst kind of problem that arises in the law is what Ronald Dworkin describes as a 'hard case'. This occurs where there are conflicting *legal* and *ethical* issues (the two different meanings of *ought*).

Ronald Dworkin's example, from his book entitled *Law's Empire*, makes this conflict perfectly clear. The law of wills in the USA says that, if a person is properly named as a beneficiary in a validly made will, that person should inherit. Fair enough. *But what if the beneficiary murdered the person who made the will?* The New York state courts had to sort that one out. The answer, you will be relieved to know, is that the murderer didn't inherit.

Both the law of wills (the murderer inherits) and the court's decision (the murderer does not inherit) seem perfectly sensible. So, do issues like this arise in UK employment law too? Yes, they do. At the time of writing, there is a case coming up in the European Court of Human Rights concerning whether the tribunals ought to apply the *standard of the reasonable employer* or apply a generalised, objective standard.

Certainly there is room for legal and political debate, but the law has to be clear and certain. What good would it do if the court said, 'Ah, that's an interesting issue', and then failed to come up with a judgment? The job of a court, especially the top courts in a legal system, is to decide an issue.

The example above has revealed something else about the law – it comes about in two ways. First there is **statute** law, which is made by Parliament, and then there is **case law**, which is judge-made law and which evolves over the years. So the law is that which Parliament says should be the law, amplified by that which judges have interpreted the law to mean. There we have it: the courts decide how to apply the law to the particular facts of a case and, at least in some circumstances, user-friendly commentaries on the law, or even ready-reckoners based on the law (God bless *tiger!*), make life simpler for non-lawyers.

It would be good if Joseph Raz recognised this as a derivative of his view that authoritative law (thou shalt do this; thou shalt not do that) is a short-cut to moral reasoning – it saves us the problem of having to think out what we should do in complex circumstances, and thus gives us time to get on with our lives. So what is this book for? It is trying to explain the (far too complex) law of employment in a user-friendly way so that you can just get on with the rest of your life.

Why has employment law become so complex? Unfortunately, it is because people try too often – at work, as well as in many other situations – to abuse relationships. The law has evolved to try to combat the abuses. In Chapter 4, we talk about the concept of mutual trust and confidence. Jesus condensed the Ten Commandments and all the intricacies of the Jewish law into 'Love God' and 'Love your neighbour'. In the same way, 'Trust one another' and 'Have confidence in one another' perfectly encapsulate the ideal employer/employee relationship. Bob thinks of the passage in the *Tao Te Ching* where the writer points out that when the Tao is absent, love and piety arise, and when love and piety fail, good and just laws arise.

A reasonable conclusion to this book might well be to remind our readers that the law is like the internal workings of a machine – we don't usually see it unless something is amiss. Employment law only comes into its own where people have failed in some way to treat each other with respect. Be glad it is there, but use it sparingly.

# Application to an Employment Tribunal

- ◆ If you fax this form you do not need to send one in the post.
- ◆ This form has to be photocopied. Please use CAPITALS and black ink (if possible).
- ◆ Where there are tick boxes, please tick to one that applies.

**1** Please give the type of complaint you want the tribunal to decide (for example, unfair dismissal, equal pay). A full list is available from the tribunal office. If you have more than one complaint list them all.

**4**

From _____ to _____

**5** Please give the name and address of the employer, other organisation or person against whom this complaint is being brought

Name _____

Address

Postcode _____

Phone number _____

Please give the place where you worked or applied to work if different from above

Address

Postcode _____

**2** Please give your details

Mr ☐  Mrs ☐  Miss ☐  Ms ☐  Other _____

First names _____

Surname _____

Date of birth _____

Address

Postcode _____

Phone number _____

Daytime phone number _____

Please give an address to which we should send documents if different from above

Postcode _____

**3** If a representative is acting for you please give details
(all correspondence will be sent to your representative)

Name _____

Address

Postcode _____

| Phone _____ | Fax _____ |
|---|---|

Reference _____

**6** Please say what job you did for the employer (or what job you applied for). If this does not apply, please say what your connection was with the employer

IT1(E/W)

7 Please give the number of normal basic hours worked each week

Hours per week

9 If your complaint is not about dismissal, please give the date when the matter you are complaining about took place

8 Please give your earning details

Basic wage or salary

£          :                    per

Average take home pay

£          :                    per

Other bonuses or benefits

£          :                    per

10 Unfair dismissal applicants only

Please indicate what you are seeking at this stage, if you win your case

☐ Reinstatement: to carry on working in your old job as before (an order for reinstatement normally includes an award of compensation for loss of earnings).

☐ Re-engagement: to start another job or new contract with your old employer (an order for re-engagement normally includes an award of compensation for loss of earnings).

☐ Compensation only: to get an award of money.

11 Please give details of your complaint

If there is not enough space for your answer, please continue on a separate sheet and attach it to this form.

12 Please sign and date this form, then send it to the appropriate address on the back cover of this booklet (see postcode list on pages 13-16).

Signed

Date

IT1/F/W)

# Useful contacts

The *tiger* website contains useful interactive advice on a number of issues of employment law: www.tiger.gov.uk.

The Department of Trade and Industry has a useful website covering a number of issues in employment law: www.dti.gov.uk/employment/index.htm will get you directly into the employment website.

## Employment tribunals

All the forms and booklets are available at your local Job Centre, or access the website.

www.employmenttribunals.gov.uk

This website enables you to submit a form IT1 online: www.employmenttribunals.gov.uk/england/forms/IT1.asp.

To receive the booklet that explains **employment tribunals**, call the Customer Services Team on 0161 833 6314.

Public enquiry line: tel 0845 795 9775.

## Discrimination

### The Equal Opportunities Commission

www.eoc.org.uk

### The Commission for Racial Equality

www.cre.gov.uk

## The Disability Rights Commission

Tel 0845 762 2633

www.drc-gb.org

## Redundancy Payment Helpline

Tel 0500 848 489

## Children and young people at work

### The Children's Legal Centre

O1206 873820

## National Minimum Wage Helpline

Tel 0845 8450 360

## General help and advice

### The National Association of Citizens Advice Bureaux

www.nacab.org.uk

### The Health & Safety Executive

www.hse.gov.uk

## Trade Unions

The Trades Union Congress (TUC) has a complete list of trade unions and other useful material.

www.tuc.org.uk

# Index

## Notes

# Notes

## Notes

# Notes

## Notes